JESUS THE LIBERATOR

JESUS THE LIBERATOR

ALAN WALKER

ABINGDON PRESS
Nashville
New York

Jesus the Liberator

Library of Congress Cataloging in Publication Data

WALKER, ALAN, 1911- Jesus the Liberator.
1. Meditations. I. Title.
BV4832.2.W33 248'.4 73-6804

ISBN 0-687-20199-3

MANUFACTURED BY THE PARTHENON PRESS AT NASHVILLE, TENNESSEE, UNITED STATES OF AMERICA

CONTENTS

1. JESUS MAKES YOU FREE

Jesus was the freest man who ever lived.

Look at his story. The Spirit of Jesus moved with supreme liberty in a large, large world. No guilt or remorse tied him to the past. No inner compulsion placed him in a prison house of self. No outer threat or pressure tyrannized him. No fear or anxiety about tomorrow clouded the future. With release and gaiety, Jesus lived out his life, showing for all time what a man who is truly free looks like.

All over the world today there rises a mighty cry for freedom. In the last generation people sought inner peace, peace of mind. Now, the mood, the goal have changed. Today, one transcendent desire expresses itself: the yearning to be free.

Youth demands freedom. With lengthened hair styles, casual dress, protest marches, its rejection of conscription and war, youth stakes its claim to liberty. The Woman's Liberation movement has arrived, shaking to its foundations the male preserves of society. Moral permissiveness, however distorted a demand, represents the rejection of anything that is restrictive and conventional. Even drug-taking is a cry for release from bondages which are regarded as intolerable.

The same cry for freedom lies behind much of the world upheaval of recent years. No people, from New Guinea to Bangladesh, from Ireland to Rhodesia, from Czechoslovakia to Vietnam, will be subject to any other people. Freedom as a ferment has undermined kings and governments, has brought empires tumbling down.

Jesus makes you free. This is the tremendous claim of the Bible. From the beginning to the end of the story, he is presented as the world's greatest liberator. Jesus, free himself, offers freedom to all the world. He came to set the captives free. "Where the Spirit of the Lord is, there is liberty." "If the Son makes you free, you will be free indeed."

The freedom Jesus offers is a gift of God. Life's liberty is not our own creation. It is the free, unmerited, unbelievable gift of God.

Science has never been able to discover how freedom entered creation. From where has come the power of choice? Neither the physicist nor the psychologist has an explanation.

No matter how far back toward the most simple forms of life you go, some rudimentary freedom is there. The biologist says even in the single cell of primitive life there is some power of choice. In man, some have suggested that freedom has entered through something's being a little loose in the brain—whatever that may mean.

What all this means is that freedom is part of God's creation. This is the way God made his world, the way he meant it to be. We were fashioned for freedom.

Then something went wrong. Man made false choices, using his freedom to set himself over against God. So sin entered. With sin came anxiety, inner compulsions, imprisonment within the self, the loss of freedom. Soon all people, though born free, were everywhere in chains.

God a second time acted for freedom's sake. In Jesus, God offered a new burst of freedom. Jesus came as a liberator to set the human spirit free. Through his life, death, and resurrection, man's lost freedom was restored.

As we open our hearts to Jesus, inner freedom comes to us. It is not found by self-effort, it is not by trusting to false substitutes for God; it is through surrender to his love and power we find our lost freedom. Gifts can only be received. As we reach out our hands toward God, so, through Christ, the freedom gift comes to us.

Let me offer a personal testimony. While on holiday on Norfolk Island, I awoke before dawn anxious and depressed. I arose and climbed to the peak of Mount Pitt which dominates the island and watched the sunrise. As the sun rose, the light spread down from the hills into the shaded valleys. Presently, even the western clouds were touched to beauty, reflecting the sun in the east.

Soon an island, bathed in light, became a symbol of a changed mood in my heart. Almost suddenly there came an elevation of spirit; a joy, a peace flooded into my heart. One by one the promises of the Bible came true: "He brought me out of a horrible pit, out of the miry clay, and set my feet upon a rock." "My grace is sufficient for you." I found myself singing: "New every morning is the grace our waking and uprising prove;" "Amazing grace, how sweet the sound, that saved a wretch like me." Suddenly the whole world was full of light. I was free.

The freedom Jesus gives remains. His gift, his presence are never withdrawn, never exhausted. Jesus makes us free, permanently.

Any freedom based on less than God sooner or later is lost. This is the tragedy of drugs and alcohol. Each seems to give release, an inner sense of liberty. Yet how temporary is the deliverance. Soon more and more alcohol and ever more potent drugs are needed to produce the same results. A recent study shows most heroin users started with alcohol. The end of the road is not freedom, but a terrible, terrible bondage.

The freedom Jesus gives, while we keep our trust in him, never fades, never disappoints. In our eyes he may change with the years, but freedom grows. Jesus meets us as teen-agers and young adults, in the mid-years and as life moves towards its close. Not even death can trap us, for at the end we go free, free for eternity.

Here is a story out of the past which shows that no inner fear, no outer pressure can crush the freedom Jesus gives.

In the third century, there lived in the imperial palace in Rome a page boy named Alexamenos. Apparently, Alexamenos was a Christian. On a wall in the quarters of the imperial pages of the palace, a crude drawing has been uncovered.

The figure of a boy is shown with hand upraised in worship, before a crucified man shown with the head of an ass. Below are the words: "Alexamenos worships his God." Underneath the drawing, in another style of handwriting, are further words: "Alexamenos is faithful."

Imagination can complete the story. Here was a slave boy brave, free enough in spirit openly to follow Jesus even in Caesar's palace. He was free enough to withstand the jeering of his fellow pages and the might of Rome.

I find this old story strangely significant. It has been repeated ten thousand times since in history. From Peter to Bonhoeffer, from Paul to Martin Luther King, Jr., we see no bonds can bind the Christian. Like Alexamenos, the Christian finds Jesus gives freedom without limit. "If the Son makes you free, you will be free indeed."

The freedom Jesus gives means responsibility. It involves a challenge to pass on to others, to seek to fashion in the structure of society, the liberty pattern of Jesus.

Jesus was free for his neighbor. Nothing could stop him from being himself, from reaching out hands to all in any form of need. He was relaxed, released no matter what happened. No rebuff sent him back within himself. No strength of prejudice or entrenched evil blocked his trying to move to the side of those who cried out for freedom. Jesus was forever free for his neighbor's sake.

Freedom is not something to enjoy, it is something to share. The gift of freedom drives us to change anything anywhere which restricts the freedom of others. To claim to be free and not be passionate in the struggle to rid the earth of racism, poverty, war—any form of oppressin—is to reveal we are not truly free.

Freedom begins within, but it works out into society. If ever this were demonstrated for all to see it is in the Pitcairn story.

To the lonely Pitcairn Island in the Pacific there came, nearly two hundred years ago, nine of the men responsible for the mutiny on their ship, *Bounty*, together with some Tahitian men and women. There they settled, but the small community was almost destroyed by the dread power of unleashed sex and alcohol. In nine years on that island there were twelve murders, one suicide, and one accidental death. Presently, only one man from the *Bounty* remained, John Adams.

One day John Adams found in a chest from the ship, a Bible. When he began reading it, a miracle happened: the new life of God came into his heart. John Adams turned from his old ways and began to teach the women and children who remained the Christian faith.

The island was transformed. In his book, *The Pitcairners,* R. B. Nicolson makes the following judgment: "After being involved in brawls, mutiny, murders, immorality and drunkenness, the last surviving mutineer turned to religion. This undoubtedly saved the island community from complete disintegration." Two hundred years later, the forces released from the heart of God still flow through the lives and society of the Pitcairners.

Freedom within can create a new society in which freedom can live and grow. "If the Son makes you free, you will be free indeed."

The freedom Jesus gives is a personal possession. Jesus sets us free one by one.

Millions today are living beneath their freedom potential. So many of us have never tasted of the freedom Jesus supplies. We live out our days in a crippling bondage to self. We are always looking over our shoulders and straining our ears to what others are saying because we have never broken free from public opinion. Unnamed, superstitious fears lurk in our minds. We are prisoners to some compulsive habit which has been built up over the years. Hence, we live strained, up-tight lives, robbed of the gaiety which only true freedom can give.

The poet Robert Frost put his finger on the cause of our inner bondage:

> Something we were withholding left us weak
> Until we found out it was ourselves.

Only as we hand over our lives to Jesus Christ shall we find the secret of liberty. Through surrender to him, we appropriate his freedom, making it our own.

In 1967, the Life Line Centre which operates Sydney's twenty-four-hour-a-day telephone counseling ministry, was partially destroyed by fire. Later, a young man was tried and sentenced for starting a number of fires, one being at Life Line.

Over five years later, following a radio broadcast service which I conducted in the Lyceum Theatre, Sydney, I received the following moving letter:

> I am writing to you for a number of reasons. Would you forgive me for the crime I committed in setting fire to the Life Line Centre in August, 1967? I have prayed to the Lord for forgiveness and feel he has forgiven me, but pray you will forgive me as well. I was listening to your program on Sunday night when you were preaching on evil spirits, and I broke down in tears when you asked new believers to come forward after the sermon. I felt I would also have liked to come forward had I been there. My sentence terminates on July 17, 1974.

In that letter is a glimpse of the freedom Jesus gives. A man is in prison, but his spirit has been released, set free by forgiveness. Somehow, he has found the freedom which is an inner personal possession.

There is a freedom which Jesus gives: personal, releasing, wonderful. It comes as we bind to ourselves the free Spirit of Jesus. Surrender to him is the key to discovery.

Jesus is—the Liberator.

2. FREEDOM FROM FEAR

In Southeast Asia, Jesus is not so much a savior from sin as a liberator from fear. This is one of the discoveries made in a mission which I conducted in Malaysia and Singapore. People in many places of Asia walk in terror of evil spirits. Black magic is prevalent. People spend time and money and effort to ward off, to placate the evil spirits that they think surround their lives impinging on them, destroying them. In this climate, the Christian missionary, the Christian preacher does forever proclaim the wonderful message: "Look, Jesus, Savior from fear."

The Christian faith was born in the first century partly as an answer to fear. Anybody who knows anything of the ancient world recognizes that the ancient world was always afraid. Therefore, it is at the very field of Bethlehem that you get the glimpse of Jesus grappling with fear for the angel said: "Be not afraid."

Somebody has calculated that the two words "fear not" are found 365 times in the Bible. The Bible is a book which grapples with fear. Jesus is presented as one who could cast out demons, who had dominance over devils, who brought deliverance to people caught in the bondage of fear.

In the later New Testament, the same theme is constantly repeated. In Paul, for example, you hear a phrase about Jesus being set far above all principalities and powers in heavenly places. This does not mean what we think it means. In Paul's day, people believed there were seven layers of air between earth and the sky and that in each of those seven layers particular species of demons lived that could suddenly plunge down, almost like modern dive bombers, and bring destruction to people and to communities. So when Paul says Christ was placed high above principalities and powers, he is declaring that Jesus is dominant over devils.

In the matchless Epistle of John, the epistle of love, the writer gives us the tremendous vision of love casting out fear. "There is no fear in love, but perfect love casts out fear." Jesus, says the whole Christian message, is a savior from fear.

I suppose you are saying: What has this got to do with us today? We do not believe in demons and evil spirits. I wonder?

There is quite a revival of the occult in the Western world. Black magic is now not unknown. There are many people who do walk in fear of evil spirits. This of course can be expected. The alternative to religious faith is not irreligion or agnosticism, it is superstition. Therefore, as faith declines in some lives, people are beginning again to be plagued by the fear of the unknown, to be haunted by evil spirits.

Peter Drucker has a powerful chapter in one of his books which is headed: "The Return of the Demons." He is not talking about evil spirits as in New Testament times. He sees in the great impersonal forces of unemployment, of the sudden eruption of war, of the violence which stalks the earth, forces which are beyond rational control. People see them almost as demons, as dread forces which can destroy their lives, in whose grip they are helpless. So Drucker talks about the return of the demons and the millions today who walk in terror of these great forces that appear to be beyond man's control.

Hence we are not talking only about Southeast Asia when we say all people need Jesus as a savior from fear. Bernard Shaw says there is only one universal passion: it is fear. Whether it is universal or not, everyone of us knows what it is to be frightened, frightened of life and frightened of death. We all have our moments when fear takes charge of our lives. To all of us comes a relevant message: "Look, Jesus, Savior from fear."

Perfect love casts out fear. How does Jesus do it? How does Jesus become the Savior from fear in Malaysia or Singapore or in any modern city?

Jesus liberates us from fear by showing us a good God whose love can be trusted. In our society, all of us take the love of God for granted. We all have absorbed the mood that this is a good world, that basically it can be trusted in the regularity of its laws, and that there are many benign forces that work around us.

Where do we get this picture of a reliable, a good world? We get it, of course, from Jesus Christ. Only Jesus has really taught us that God is love. This is what we learn when we come face to face with other world religions. We live by the Christian conception of God. God is love, God is good, and all he has made is good.

In Malaysia it is very different. Someone gets sick and it is thought to be the work of an evil spirit that has somehow entered the house. Therefore, the spirit must be placated. Gifts must be made. Somehow the spirit must be driven away.

As you move along highways in Malaysia, you will find little shrines at curves in the road. There, at that bend, perhaps somebody has not been able to negotiate the curve and has crashed into a tree and been killed. That would be our explanation. Their explanation is that an evil spirit lives at that bend of the road, and it pushed that car into the tree. So a shrine is built to stop further disasters. The spirit must be placated so that it will not push another car into the tree.

Or consider the girl born in a Chinese home in Malaysia. She turns out to be a very pretty little girl and she has a name given to her. But the family presently begins to call her "Piglet." She grows up with the name "Piglet." And you say, what an unkind thing to do to a little girl to liken her to a pig.

Why? People believe that very handsome and gifted persons might attract the attention of the evil spirits and therefore they must be tricked. The real name is not used; if an evil spirit gets to know that name, it can get power over you. So the family calls a little girl "Piglet," hoping they will trick the spirit into thinking the child is ugly and not pretty.

Evil spirits are the cause of death. So death is surrounded with ceremonies that are so many attempts to drive away evil spirits.

What about us, in our Western culture? Here we do know that God is love. There is tremendous deliverance for men and women in the simple truth that you and I, all people, are deeply and personally loved by God, our heavenly Father, and we are held constantly, always, in the hollow of his hand. If we believe this, we begin to conquer fear, and without it fear conquers us.

Some time ago I read the story of a woman who lived at the time of the American Civil War when the North and South forces advanced and retreated around her home. Sometimes it passed under the control of the Northern army, sometimes of the Southern army. One day she rose from bed in the morning and was just getting breakfast when she heard gunfire outside. Presently a group of soldiers came in—enemy soldiers to her, for she was of the North—and they demanded breakfast.

When the breakfast was ready, she turned to the enemy soldiers and said: "It is a custom of long standing in this home that we always have prayers before we eat our breakfast. I hope you will not mind if we have prayers today." So she took down her Bible and she read Psalm 27: "The Lord is my light and my salvation; whom shall I fear? The Lord is the stronghold of my life; of whom shall I be afraid?"

The soldiers were very quiet as she read, and then she bowed her head and began to pray. While her eyes were closed, she heard some movement round the room. At the close of the prayer, she opened her eyes and found the soldiers were gone. The enemy had silently crept away.

I think that is a parable of what Jesus Christ does. If we believe that God is love, that the Lord is our light and our salvation, the enemy fear creeps away. So, Jesus, Savior from fear, comes to us because in power he gives us the picture that God is love, God is good, God can be trusted. In this faith, we can live and conquer fear. "There is no fear in love, but perfect love casts out fear."

Jesus is Savior because in his presence he is able to entice us to bring our fears out into the open. He draws them to the surface, either through confession or by the intimate sharing which comes with praying. We gain release because we face our fears and look at them in his presence.

Fear is a blackmailer. Fear hurts us most when it remains in the shadows, when its true nature and purpose are hidden from us. Every one of us is in some sense the victim of conscious and unconscious fears that we have buried in our life.

Lord Soper tells the story of a friend of his who was a very sane and balanced person but who had an unreasonable fear of dogs. Whenever he walked along a road and a dog barked, he almost turned and ran. This really troubled him that he should so foolishly cringe before a mere dog.

This man went to see a psychologist. Presently, in conversation, as he probed into the past, the psychologist came upon a forgotten memory. Apparently, when this man was only a baby about ten months old, he had been taken down the road in a carriage by his mother; and a boisterous, but quite friendly dog suddenly jumped into the carriage, causing the child to scream with fear. Here was the origin of that unreasonable fear of dogs. Because a skillful counselor was able to bring a forgotten memory out into the open, bring it to the surface, it was robbed of its power to hurt. So Lord Soper says, "My friend no longer fears dogs."

Many of us, of course, have quite conscious fears which we cannot control. I do not know what your fears are. I like the story of the little fellow who said to his father one day: "Daddy, are you afraid of cows?" "Oh no, son," said his father. "Are you afraid of woolly worms?" "Oh, of course not, son." "Well," he said, "you aren't afraid of anybody except Mummy, are you?"

I do not know what are your personal fears, but everyone, if honest, would admit to some. Here is a list of common fears: fear of disease, perhaps most of all of cancer; fear of unemployment, especially as we get older; fear of losing a wife or a husband or a child; fear as parents of the possible birth of an abnormal child; fear of loneliness; fear of responsibility, that you might be asked to do more than you can; fear of failure in a success culture. Above all, there is the unmentionable fear, fear of death.

What is your fear? Perhaps I have not named it, but there will be some fears lurking in all our lives, many of them known to no one but ourselves, and to God.

What are we to do with our fears? We stop them from blackmailing us. We bring them out into the open. We talk to some trusted minister or friend. In prayer we lay them out before God.

It is time we remembered the tremendous therapy there is in prayer. In the intimate moment of prayer we can breathe out in God's presence anxieties and fears we would not even mention to a close friend or loved one.

I wonder whether you have learned what prayer can mean as the place where the mask falls and where fears, which perhaps only strike in the middle of the night, are faced in God's presence and power. I wonder whether you have prayed about your fears, confessing them to God, lately.

Over in Penang, we had a tremendous meeting in the city hall as the climax of the Mission to Malaysia. After the service, I made an appeal inviting people to commit their lives openly to Jesus Christ. One man who came forward was almost seventy years of age. His hair was white, he was a little stooped as he walked.

Afterwards, he came to me and he said: "Mr. Walker, you are going back to Australia tomorrow, but I wonder would you pray for me. For years I have been followed by an evil spirit. He has done many, many bad things to me, and I cannot shake him off. Tonight I think I have moved ahead of that spirit, and he will not be able to catch up with me any more. Now I have given my life to Jesus, I believe I will shake off that evil spirit, but please pray for me, Mr. Walker, pray that the evil spirit will never catch up with me again."

Let me ask a pointed question. Do you pray that your fears shall not catch up with you ever again and that you, with calmness and quietness of mind, will rest your life in Jesus Christ as Savior from fear? "There is no fear in love, but perfect love casts out fear."

Jesus is a liberator from fear because he is the embodiment of perfect love.

Paul Tournier makes this claim: "Fear is not amenable to the will. We can repress it, but not liquidate it; we can compromise with it, but that is no victory."

We can say also that fear is not amenable to reason. How many times have we told ourselves, I'm silly to fear that, but then a few hours later, a few days later, we are as full of fear as ever. Fear is not amenable to rational argument, nor does it respond to a firm act of the will.

Fear, you see, is an emotion and an emotion is not controlled by mind or by will. An emotion can only be dealt with by another emotion. This is what the Bible is talking about. Perfect love casts out fear, not perfect knowledge; perfect love casts out fear. Only as we live in an atmosphere surrounded by love, only as we let the greater love of God come into our hearts can we really handle the emotion called fear.

Love is a stronger emotion than fear. Because love and fear are incompatible, the more love comes in, the more fear subsides. This is why two people, as they come to know each other and love each other more, fear each other less. Love swallows up fear as it grows stronger.

Here is an incident which illustrates the power of love. It happened at Marburg in Germany. A mother was at a circus with a little girl who suddenly slipped out of her sight and disappeared. The next moment her mother saw that the child had pressed through the bars of the lion's cage in the circus. There she was, next to the lion in the cage. The lion already had its claws near the child. The mother, without a moment's hesitation, rushed to the door of the cage and threw it open. She went into the lion's cage, she grasped the child in her arms, brought her out, slammed the door of the cage in the lion's face, and fainted.

Now, that woman feared a lion as much as you and I do, but for the moment love cast out fear. Because of her love of her child she was able to face a lion, for the moment, unafraid. That is what love can do. When it is strong enough, love casts out fear.

There is only one place in all the world where the fullness, the perfection of love is found. It is in the love of God. It is in Jesus Christ. It is at a place called Calvary where Jesus Christ died for you and me.

God so loved the world he gave his only Son for us and for all people. Whether it is in Malaysia or Sydney, it is as we open our hearts to more and more of the love of God that fear is driven away.

The trouble with so many of us is that we have not yet found perfect love. We have not yet discovered the perfect expression of love which is found only in one person, Jesus Christ, and only in one place, the Cross on which he died.

Only as we allow the perfect love of God to take charge of us will fear be swallowed up in victory. Only as we approach the cross of Jesus and allow the wonder of his love to seep into the very depths of our imagination and our emotion, does Jesus become Liberator from fear. "There is no fear in love, but perfect love casts out fear."

3. DELIVERED FROM LONELINESS

I wonder if there has ever been a lonelier man than Jesus. Earlier than most of us at the age of twelve, he moved beyond his parents' thought and understanding. Through his life, he walked a solitary way. The men who understood him best only half understood him. His family wanted once to take him quietly home, questioning his sanity. Soon his followers thinned out, and he asked of those who remained: "Will you also go away?" At the end, deserted, betrayed, he stood entirely alone. Was there ever anyone lonelier than Jesus?

Loneliness today is a great modern sickness of soul. The nature of society has changed. In the Middle Ages, people huddled together for there was little privacy even among the rich. Family circles were closely knit. Now all is changed. Society has disintegrated the life of the people. Now amid the lonely crowd, millions live in isolation and loneliness of spirit.

How, how can loneliness be overcome? How can we all claim a sense of belonging? Does Jesus liberate us from the sorrows of being alone?

Human beings were created to stand alone. The splendid isolation of everyone is a mark of humanity.

Jesus was never so great as when he stood alone, one man against the world. Jesus chose aloneness. Nowhere is it recorded he sought advice of his disciples. Never did he make compromises in order to be understood or to move nearer to people. He walked and died alone. Jesus learned to live with this loneliness. Once he said: "The hour is coming, . . . when you will be scattered, . . . and will leave me alone; yet I am not alone, for the Father is with me."

The famous preacher Robertson of Brighton says of Jesus, "Look at the grandeur of the Spirit of Jesus. Compassion! Compassion for Him! Adore Him if you will, respect and reverence that sublime solitariness—but no pity."

Let us then start with the uniqueness, the greatness of loneliness. Human nature was designed so that we could retreat within ourselves and be satisfied. From isolation, from the individual integrity of our own lives, we then are free to move into relationships with others. There is a price to be paid for togetherness. We were meant for solitary splendor. We were meant to travel, if necessary alone, the white road of conscience. You and I were made for solitude.

Much is often made of the loneliness of people who live in the densely crowded apartment areas of big cities. What is often forgotten is that people want it this way. They do not want to be involved with their neighbors, preferring to choose friends at a distance. They have no desire to get caught up in fellowship or community groups either of a secular kind or in the neighborhood church. It almost seems they say with a certain famous actress, "I want to be alone."

Nothing is more impressive in the life of the former Secretary-General of United Nations, Dag Hammarskjöld, than his splendid isolation, his accepted loneliness of spirit. His very greatness derived in part from his readiness to remain detached, his acceptance of solitude.

We catch a glimpse of the spirit of Dag Hammerskjöld in words like these: "A mature man is his own judge; a man of firm convictions does not ask for understanding from those with whom he comes into conflict." We see something of the origin of this lonely independence of mind in his admiration of Jesus whom he described as "a young man, adamant in His commitment, who walks the road of possibility to the end without self-pity."

Let us begin here. Loneliness can be a mark of greatness.

Human beings are made for fellowship. This too must be said. As an early church statement reads, "The man who keeps to himself cannot be made whole."

Jesus cried out for friends. He chose twelve men to be with him. He had an inner circle of three of his disciples, and one was his special friend who "lay on His bosom." Jesus made friends easily. Once, for example, he was willing to risk his life because Mary, Martha, and their brother Lazarus needed him at Bethany. In the Garden of Gethsemane he took his men to be with him and had close at hand his three best friends.

Out of Christ's understanding of the need of all people for friendship, came his great gift of the church. The time has come to realize the tremendous vision that Jesus had when he set out to create communities of people called the church set down in every part of the world. The purpose of the church is to offer fellowship, and splendidly in many places it does. It is cheap and popular today to deride the church. The wonder, the beauty of the church in modern society should be grasping our minds. Millions find in the church on the corner a community of sharing people, a place where every individual counts. No one will ever be able to calculate how many people are made and kept whole because the church is their fellowship.

I read of a letter recently which emphasized how fortunate most of us are in being set within the circle of a family, of relatives. It said: "I am so glad I have relations, brothers and sisters and cousins, for I know some people who haven't any."

There are many such. The church for people like this becomes a place of spiritual relatives. I have seen it happen a hundred times. In the fellowship of the followers of Jesus, a substitute family has been found, a family of concern, of caring, of love. It is, I suspect, what Jesus meant his church to be.

The wonder of the church is also seen in its universal quality. Today with millions of people traveling and many others moving from land to land, there is need of a society of people which is found everywhere, which does not stop at national boundaries.

I can only speak of the church as I find it. It has been my lot to travel far and often. It has meant everything at times in some foreign, lonely place to find the church there. To be accepted at once as a member of Christ's people, to encounter something familiar in ideas, in music, in subtle overtones of relationship has been to conquer loneliness.

Recently in Sydney, Australia, we had a dramatic happening which showed the reality of the universal nature of the caring community called the church. As part of the outreach of the Central Methodist Mission, a round-the-clock telephone ministry called Life Line was established.

One night, a distraught call came to the Life Line Centre from a father whose daughter had just telephoned him from Washington, D.C. She had rung to say good-bye, stating that life was no longer worth living and she had in her hand tablets which she said she would take.

Knowing not what to do, the father rang Life Line. At once, the trans-Pacific lines were cleared to rush through a call to a Methodist minister in Washington. A second call to the police was made. Within half an hour, both the minister and the police arrived at the girl's apartment. They arrived in time to save her life. She was taken to the minister's home, counseling help was gained for her. Weeks later, a grateful family, re-united in Sydney, called the Life Line to express a simple thank you.

The presence of a universal fellowship in today's world is more necessary than ever in history. Human loneliness, human needs do not stop at national boundaries. Under God for such a time as this, the universal church has come into being. It is part of God's answer to the isolation, the aloneness of people all over the world.

The answer to friendlessness is to be a friend. As Emerson once said, "The only way to have a friend is to be a friend."

I remember an amusing incident in our family when the children were young. One night there was a terrific storm, the lightning flashed, the thunder roared. One of the children awoke and, thinking he would be frightened, I brought him into my bed. Presently when there was a particularly deafening clap of thunder I took my son's hand in mine. His response was, "Are you frightened, Daddy?"

If only we would reach out a hand to people around us we would be amazed at the response. Back would come the query: Are you lonely too? The answer would be yes, and in giving friendship we would find our own hearts warmed with companionship.

How varied are the forms of loneliness around us. Each reveals its own nature and requires its own answer.

There is the loneliness of children. Henry Lawson, the poet, tells how, as a child, he would be desperately lonely and go off on his own to cry behind the barn on the family farm. He describes how sometimes as he cried his dog would come with slobbering sympathy, and he would bury his wet face in the dog's shaggy hair and gain comfort.

There is the loneliness of sickness. There are the long hours when nobody comes to visit, the anxiety over the cost of sickness and how bills are to be paid, the worry over the future. No wonder John Donne wrote: "As sickness is the greatest misery, so the greatest misery of sickness is solitude."

There is the loneliness of sin. Sin separates us from our fellows and from God. Coleridge expresses this truth in his epic poem, *The Ancient Mariner*. The mariner, convinced he had committed a serious sin, says:

> O Wedding Guest! this soul hath been
> Alone on a wide wide sea:
> So lonely 'twas that God himself
> Scarce seemed there to be.

There is the loneliness of circumstances, of isolation, as in the Australian outback where sometimes houses are five hundred miles apart. There is the loneliness of cities.

Albert Camus asks, "Do you know what the solitary creature is like as he wanders in great cities?"

During the last war, a small boy, whose parents had been killed in Burma, and a doctor's wife, whose husband had died, were thrown together on a ship moving back toward America. One day, the lonely boy said to the woman: "You and I are the only Americans on the ship." Trapped in her own sorrow, the woman brushed him to one side.

The ship was torpedoed, the woman and the boy escaping with several others in a life boat. For days, they tossed on the ocean, each one in the boat fighting for life. It was then that the boy turned again to the woman. This time, she said, "He came to me shivering like a terrified little bird. He needed me."

So, the two lonely people clung together until the rescue. A relationship began between the sorrowing widow and the orphaned boy. Both found strength in their companionship and the friendship which persisted when they were safely back in America. Later, people who knew them, said it was hard to say which saved which. Each found a new power in offering something to the other. The only way to have a friend is to be a friend.

Human beings are made for fellowship with God. As Jesus said, "I am not alone, for the Father is with me."

Nothing is more impressive in the life of Jesus than his friendship with God. Always he was stepping into the presence of God, finding there an answer to his loneliness of spirit, finding a companionship which gave him courage to endure.

"Religion," says Professor Whitehead, "is what a man does with his solitariness." It is a true definition. Anyone who discovers the reality of God discovers the reality of an inner companionship. God appears to those who seek him; as the hymn says, "God leads the lonely home."

The Christian faith declares that, in spite of the vastness of space, God cares for every man and woman. The Christian faith says that, in spite of the vastness of the human family, every person counts. Each one of us can say, "I am not alone, for the Father is with me."

Earlier in this century, a Christian minister, known affectionately as Dick Shepherd, was rector of St. Martin's-in-the-Field in London. Presently, in the life of Dick Shepherd, a deep sorrow developed. His wife turned to another man, and he was left alone. He continued to live alone in the large rectory which had been their home. Often, it is said that after some great meeting in which he had poured out his mind and heart in an effort to win the peace, to establish justice, or to offer men Christ, he would return and find only emptiness.

One night, his biographer tells, he came home late and felt he could not enter his dark and lonely house. Turning from the door, he went to a nearby club where he was a member. He climbed the stairs to a small room which he knew was mostly deserted. There, far into the night, he sat with his thoughts, trying to pray. He looked out across the now-deserted Trafalgar Square, and presently he was almost overcome with loneliness. Dropping his head on his hands on a table, he prayed simply, "Jesus, Jesus, be to me a Jesus and save me." And Jesus did! Next day, he was back in the fight with faith and courage renewed.

In Sydney, we worship every Sunday night in the Lyceum in the heart of the theater district. It becomes on Sunday a unique church-in-a-theater. As people leave the service of worship, they see a sign written above the doorway, "Remember I am with you always."

In that message is the Christian answer to loneliness. In the friendship of Jesus is deliverance from loneliness.

4. DEFEATING DEFEAT

There is a haunting dread in the lives of many of us modern men and women. It is fear of failure and defeat. Society mercilessly throws at us the dream of success written in terms of affluence, bodily beauty, and personal acceptance. Inevitably many, falling short of achievement, must learn to live with a sense of disappointment and defeat.

In the Bible there is a man called Peter. He experienced many a setback, many a defeat. Yet, through it all, he became liberated from the fact and the fear of personal failure. Through all that happened, the Spirit of Jesus fashioned a life of real freedom and greatness.

We know more about Simon, whom Jesus renamed Peter, than most people mentioned in the Bible. We are therefore able to watch him find release and growth. He falls to rise, grows in character from instability to steadfastness, moves from being a humble fisherman to the leader of the disciple band which Jesus established and eventually of the early church.

How did Peter overcome defeat? By what means did

Jesus lead his spirit out until he triumphed over weaknesses within his life and the obstacles he faced around him?

All begins with the vision of possibilities which we accept in our own lives. The image we build up in ourselves can carry us downward or lead us onward.

Jesus apparently saw great potential in Simon Peter. It was his brother Andrew who brought Simon to Jesus and He immediately saw in the rugged fisherman before him, not the man Simon was, but the man by God's grace he could become.

To Simon, Jesus gave the name Peter, "rocklike." Yet nothing was further from the truth. Simon was unsteady, mercurial. He was capable of flashes of courage and boisterous loyalty—and abject betrayal. Jesus never wavered in his faith in Peter. So at the end, after the denial and desertion of the Crucifixion, Peter earned his new name; he became rocklike. This was finally proved in the crisis of his death and his steadfastness to the point of martyrdom.

I have come to believe that the self-image we accept goes far toward determining the kind of person we become. For someone to believe in us, to encourage us, helps greatly in personality growth. If we have a clear image of the kind of person we desire to be, we will struggle on through defeat to triumph.

Through someone's setting up impossible goals Jenny Lind, the "Swedish Nightingale," presently was enchanting the world with her matchless voice. Jenny Lind was an orphan who was brought up by a woman in poor circumstances in Stockholm. While she was away at work, this woman would lock Jenny in her room. To fill in the long, dreary hours, Jenny used to sing to herself while looking out of the window.

One day, as an old music teacher was passing he heard her singing. Next day, he brought a friend to listen, and they agreed she had a voice of tremendous possibilities. These two men became her guardians, and gradually, by much encouragement, they drew out the wonderful latent gift which was in her. In time, she began to sing in operas in Europe, England, and America. The world was at her feet.

As the years passed, something even more significant than her glorious voice developed in Jenny Lind. It was a personality of deep Christian piety and grace. All occurred because someone had believed in her, someone gave to her a vision of what could be and encouraged her to achieve it.

Defeating defeat depends on accepting the wonder of forgiveness. Without the creative power of forgiveness, we often lack the hope and the courage to fight back after failure.

The story of the meeting between Jesus and Peter beside the Sea of Galilee after the Resurrection is one of the most tender and delicate studies in human relationships in all literature. In it we see Jesus building up faith and hope in a defeated man.

Peter had collapsed morally before the pressures of the crucifixion of Jesus. In the Garden of Gethsemane, when the soldiers moved to arrest Jesus, Peter turned and ran. Before a charcoal fire in Pilate's judgment hall, as a rooster twice crowed in the early morning, Peter three times denied Jesus. At once, overwhelmed with guilt, he went out and wept bitterly.

Then Jesus let loose the processes of redemption. To a man who thought he had excluded himself forever from the fellowship of his friends, Jesus sent a special message, Go tell my disciples and Peter I shall meet them in Galilee.

In Galilee, Peter again found Jesus beside a charcoal fire. Three times Peter had denied Jesus, so three times the question is asked: "Do you love me?" At the end of the conversation, Jesus challenges Peter with the same words as at the beginning of his ministry, "Follow me."

Jesus, with great skill, forces Peter to face the facts of his defeat. They must not be buried in the subconscious before their power to haunt and destroy has been taken away by frankness and forgiveness.

Many of our inner personal defeats are, in our own eyes, moral defeats. Something has happened in secret or openly which has represented a collapse of our highest standards. Impurity, jealousy, bitterness, cupidity have challenged us, and we succumbed. Therefore, defeating defeat means grasping the wonder of God's forgiveness.

What a liberation of spirit comes with forgiveness. Most of us can tell of the kind of experience which came recently to me.

In exhaustion, I had fallen far below the standards which are part of a Christian profession. I felt excluded, alienated from the grace of God. In distress, I sat at a piano and began flicking over the pages of a hymn book, playing restlessly tune after tune. Suddenly, one of Charles Wesley's hymns spoke to me with power. I found myself singing with gathering assurance and joy:

> Depth of mercy! can there be
> Mercy still reserved for me? . . .
> There for me the Savior stands,
> Holding forth his wounded hands;
> God is love! I know, I feel,
> Jesus weeps and loves me still.

Overcoming defeat means finding courage enough to fight again, to keep fighting. It is to believe that no defeat is final, no failure is fatal.

John Hutton says: "Don't give up yet, for everyone can hold on a little longer." This is what carries many an athlete through to victory. In a long-distance race, the breath comes in great gasps, the limbs are weary, the throat is hot and parched. Then, as though some secret reserve strength is tapped and what is called a second wind comes. At once there is new release and freedom. It is the prelude to the victor's crown.

"Everyone can hold on a little longer." That is the kind of message which carried Norman Vincent Peale through the greatest personal crisis of his life.

There developed, in the midst of his successful New York ministry, a swelling tide of criticism of the gospel he preached. It came from theologians, church leaders, and many a Christian minister. Presently, Dr. Peale felt there was but one course of action open to him: he must resign from the Christian ministry.

In the midst of this personal crisis, Dr. Peale's father became desperately ill. He rushed to his side, saying nothing, of course, of the decision he had reached to leave the church he served.

Some days later, his father died, and again Peale made the journey to his old home. In his pocket was the resignation already written, waiting to be posted. When he reached his destination, his stepmother drew him to one side.

"Your father left a message for you," she said. "Something's wrong with Norman. I can read him like a book. Tell Norman I've read every word he has written. What he says is in harmony with the basic truths of Christianity.

Tell Norman, 'Put your trust in Jesus Christ and never quit!' "

In a few moments in another room, Dr. Peale took the letter of resignation and handed it to his wife. "Tear it up," he said. Together they watched the small pieces of paper fluttering into a basket.

Defeating defeat means fighting back resolutely when everything seems lost. "Put your trust in Jesus Christ and never quit."

Overcoming defeat depends in part on a strong sense of being trusted. To realize someone is ready to give responsibility and does not expect failure is an exhilarating feeling.

Jesus used the power of an entrustment finally to restore Peter and to bind him in loyalty into the future. Along with the threefold question, "Do you love me?" three times a commission is given to Peter: "Feed my lambs," "Tend my sheep," "Feed my sheep." These words must have fallen like a glorious melody on the ears of Peter. Jesus trusts me! Jesus trusts me!

I wonder how many of us are drawn back from defeat by the thought of those who trust us. There is the intimate circle of family: husband, wife, parent, child. We cannot, must not fail them. There is the wider circle of friends, the people in the church or the community whom we do not want to betray. There is Jesus himself. Who among us who love him is ready to betray his confidence in us?

No one trusts us like Jesus. Since the first century, he has picked up men and women—often with only hidden potential—who have grown in stature and never let him down. All over the world, right now, the power of the person of Jesus is drawing young people out of themselves, entrusting to them huge tasks in which they will not fail or desert. Why? Because they are determined not to fail the One who has placed his trust in them.

There is an attractive early pioneer in Australia who became liberated by the Jesus who won his allegiance. Silas Gill was born in a Sussex village, becoming a farm laborer. He grew to be a tall and strong man, much above the average. He became locally notorious for his boxing prowess at county fairs and for his smuggling activities along the coast.

One night in 1832, Silas Gill was present at a small service in a Wesleyan chapel. At the appeal for people to hand over their lives to Jesus Christ, Silas Gill came forward. The preacher, Rev. Thomas Collins, knew him and said simply, "Here comes a giant for Jesus."

A giant Silas Gill proved to be, and not only in physical bulk. A few years later, when he migrated to Australia, he became one of the great Christian laymen who planted the Methodist Church firmly in Australian soil.

In an area forty to fifty miles from Sydney, Silas Gill settled, and at once began to gather people to hear the gospel. His biographer, Eric Clancy, says: "Silas was gloriously happy and made the countryside ring with his shouts of glory and praise. He was known to attend meetings at Quarry Grove, 16 miles distant, carrying his child in his arms, and arriving home between two and three o'clock in the morning."

Later Silas Gill moved north, spending some years along each of three rivers, the Hunter, the Hastings, and the Macleay. In each area, he earned enough by farming to keep his large family, but he lived chiefly to spread the gospel of Jesus. Each time he moved, it was not for work or economic reasons, but because he heard the call to proclaim Christ to a new region, as the pioneer people moved in, and to establish the church. The Methodist Church is today strong in these areas of Australia because Silas Gill and others like him believed they were entrusted by Christ with a great task.

A giant for Jesus! Silas Gill stood in the Peter tradition. And what a tradition it is. A man, strong, tough, with perhaps little education, but with a tremendous potential for leadership. With powers released by Jesus, they have left their mark in the history of many places in many centuries. Often failing, often recovering, they went on to greatness.

There is no limit to what Jesus can do with a life given in dedication to him. This is the fundamental miracle of Jesus, the Liberator.

5. I AM ACCEPTED

I suppose you have noticed how in today's films and in the theater the spectator is always being drawn into the action. The angle of the camera, the wide cinerama screen, the theater-in-the-round have but one purpose. It is to make you and me feel part of the drama, to force us mentally, emotionally to be involved.

There is an incident in the Bible which, more than most, draws us into the action. I defy anyone quietly to read the story of the woman taken in adultery without becoming emotionally involved.

Here is the scene. Jesus came early one morning from the Mount of Olives. At once, the crowds began to gather. All at once there is a commotion. A group of hard-faced Scribes and Pharisees drag a woman through the crowd and push her forward before Jesus.

"This woman was caught in the act of adultery. The law of Moses says stone her. What shall we do with her?"

Jesus appeared to be trapped. If he agreed to the stoning, he would break the Roman law, for the Romans did not permit Jews to carry out capital punishment. If he rejected the sentence, he was breaking Jewish law.

Stooping down, Jesus wrote on the ground. I wonder why. Was he playing for time? Was he embarrassed by the presence of the helpless woman crouching perhaps half-naked before him? I wonder what words he traced in the dust. Probably he just doodled on the soil.

Suddenly Jesus looked up. "Let him who is without sin among you be the first to cast a stone at her." Immediately, the whole incident is lifted from a legal to a moral level. With great penetration, he touches the springs of conscience in these odious men. They shuffle, they glance uneasily at one another. Then, one by one, they leave, while the crowd stands silent, watching, just watching.

Presently only Jesus and the woman remain, encircled by the crowd. "Has no one condemned you?"

"No, sir."

Then came the unforgettable words: "Neither do I condemn you. Go and sin no more."

Involved? Who can read the story without becoming emotionally part of the drama? Inevitably, we identify with the judgmentalism of the Pharisees; the neutral crowd; the isolated, lonely woman; or with Jesus, filled with compassion.

How the Scribes and Pharisees needed to be liberated from the harsh, ugly spirit which had gripped them. They show no real concern for morality. They appear to be gloating over the woman. She was caught in the very act of adultery, they say, and you can almost hear their salacious lips smacking over what they had seen.

The woman, to them, was a pawn. It was Jesus they were after, hoping to trap him into saying something which could be whipped up into a charge against him. By his skill in debate, Jesus turned the tables on his enemies. Suddenly, with themselves placed on the defensive, they retreated. Soon they had melted into the crowd, the eldest leaving first, the youngest last.

Life does strange things with us all as we grow older. Some people mellow as the years pass, becoming more gracious, more tolerant. A friend of an aged Indian woman said gushingly to her, "Oh, but you are beautiful." The answer came, "I ought to be. I have lived for eighty years."

For some, life means contraction, the dying of compassion, harshness of judgment, bigotry. The spirit of some unpleasant older people is etched unmistakably on their faces.

The Greek philosopher Aristotle talked about this kind of person, long ago. Ordinarily, Aristotle is a gentle, benign writer, but in one passage he pillories a certain type of aged person. He describes the unlovely old as human nature fallen into ruin, selfish, showing nothing but unfeeling meanness of spirit.

Anthony Bloom, Archbishop in charge of the Russian Church in London, tells of a man who said to him in London: "The story I love most in the Bible is the one about the woman taken in adultery."

"Well, let us have a look at it. If you were there, what would you have done?"

"Honestly," he replied, "I think if I had been there, I would not have walked away; I would have stayed to stone her."

Then Anthony Bloom said, "You had better pray you never fall into the hands of God."

Where do we stand? Some of us, because of the critical, judgmental spirit we show, line up with the Pharisees. The Pharisees brought a woman taken in adultery and set her in the midst.

There is another group which figures in the story. It

is the people who stand around watching, just watching.

The crowd was large. All the people came to him, it says. Near at hand were the disciples. In reading the story, you almost forget they are there. They say nothing, they show no outward reactions. Gripped, no doubt, by the drama, they remain, looking on in silence.

In the Bible the crowd often fills the role of passive watching. I think one of the ugliest sentences in literature appears in the story of the Crucifixion. As Jesus died in agony, the account says, "And the people stood by, watching."

Still, crowds just watch. From recent happenings, illustrations are easy to find. Crowds watched while some despicable Irish women shaved and tarred and feathered two girls because they showed friendship with British soldiers.

In *Time*, there appeared the terrible picture of a man being bayonetted to death in Dacca and a small boy being kicked to death by Bangladesh soldiers. Forming a circle around this happening was a crowd of people. On their faces was intense interest as they stood watching—passively—a man and a boy die.

During the long drawn-out agony of the Vietnamese War, millions of people in Australia and America just watched from afar the suffering. Leaving it to the politicians, to the soldiers—many conscripted and sent far from their homes—the people continued on their normal ways. History will record Vietnam as one of the supreme, unnecessary tragedies of the centuries, but too many of us, with our conscience and compassion drugged, just watched.

Here in Australia, we accept a racially based migration policy which excludes the friendly, attractive people of Fiji and Tonga. While the economy in these small islands cannot support growing populations, the vast land of Australia is closed to most of them. Why? Because the color of their skin is not white. Most Australians just look on, letting it happen. We form the crowd that watches, just watches.

Where do we stand in relation to the great issues of our time? Many of us would have honestly to say that in today's inescapable dramas—where right and wrong clash, where cruelty appears, where injustice flourishes, where Christ is crucified afresh—we sit and watch. Evil reigns while we say and do nothing, governed by the cowardly attitude: I do not want to get involved.

They placed the woman in the midst. There she stands, a helpless, pathetic figure. Our sympathy surely flows out toward her, a nameless woman of the city.

As the victim she seemingly has no defense. She says nothing to counter the charges made against her. She appears crushed by the judgment of others. Only once in the narrative does she speak. When Jesus asks whether anybody has condemned her, she replies, "No one, Lord."

Where do we stand? If we were fully honest, we would have to leave our safe place amid the anonymous crowd and stand beside her. We would admit to moments, thoughts, acts of sensuality. We would confess we have far to go if we are to be pure in mind and heart.

We are living in one of the most stained, sexually exploited periods of history. Few of us can escape the contamination which comes with free-flowing pornography. It meets us everywhere, on the pages of the Sunday newspaper, on the television screen, and at the movies.

How many of us honestly could do other than confess with the woman taken in adultery, "I have sinned"? Under all the stimulation of this kind of society, who would not say in penitence, "I have looked lustfully on a man or a woman"? Who would not confess there have been times when the battle for purity within has been lost? Who would not admit to a twinge of conscience when we hear the phrase: "Thou hast set . . . our secret sins in the light of thy countenance"? Some of us would have to say brokenly, our impurity of imagination has expressed itself in overt action.

No one would want to raise probing questions like these without knowing there is something beyond confession, something beyond sorrow: forgiveness. In the love and pardon of God we find hope. The matchless invitation of Isaiah comes to us:

> Come now let us reason together, . . .
> though your sins are like scarlet,
>   they shall be as white as snow;
> though they be red like crimson,
>   they shall become like wool.

The climax of the story is Jesus. At the end, all we see and hear is Jesus. There he stands saying quietly: "Neither do I condemn you. Go and sin no more."

Let this be said: No one can claim endorsement for moral permissiveness from Jesus as he appears in this story. His last word is, "Go, sin no more." Jesus does not condemn the woman. He does condemn the act of adultery as sinful; he does command a new way of life. "Go, sin no more."

Jesus with infinite delicacy and tenderness does tacitly condemn the act of adultery. Adultery, he is saying, represents serious moral failure. Adultery is an offense against purity. Adultery has within it the power to wreck a marriage, to destroy a love. There is inherent in the story endorsement of the Seventh Commandment: You shall not commit adultery.

Somehow, through it all, Jesus conveys not rejection but acceptance to a stricken woman. Undoubtedly, she went away with a new joy in her heart: I am accepted. I am not an outcast. Jesus, the prophet, has forgiven me, accepted me; I am accepted. Acceptance is the secret of moral and spiritual renewal.

Paul Tillich, in the language of a theologian, expresses what happens. "You are accepted. You are accepted, accepted by that which is greater than you. Do not try to do anything now; perhaps later you will do much. Do not seek for anything; do not perform anything; do not intend anything. Simply accept the fact that you are accepted!"

"Neither do I condemn you. Go and sin no more."

6. NO CONDEMNATION NOW

There came into my office a rather shabbily dressed, little old lady. When I tried to shake hands, she held out her left hand. I noticed then that her right arm hung limply at her side.

"Do you think I can ever be forgiven?" was her first question. Presently, slowly, her story was told. During the First World War she was married, and six days later she saw her young husband sail for the battlefields of France.

Being desperately lonely, she formed a relationship with another man soon after her husband left, hiding it from him. Letters went to and fro from France for some months, then came the news her husband had been killed in action.

Later, she married the one with whom she had been living. After forty years of marriage he died. Now she was sick and old and tired. She found she was thinking much of that first soldier husband. For her unfaithfulness, though he had known nothing about it, she now was overwhelmed with guilt.

Recently her right arm had become paralyzed. "The doctor tells me he can find nothing wrong with it. However, there is no strength in it; I cannot use my arm or hand," she said.

Then, shyly, she turned back the lapel of her coat, revealing the ribbons and decorations sent to her following her first husband's death. "Do you think God could ever forgive me for what I did to him?" she asked again. I tried to tell her of the wonder of the love and forgiveness of God. As we talked, she seemed to grasp it all. I explained that it was for people just like her that Jesus came and on the Cross died as our Savior. We prayed together. Then, in a firm voice, I dared to pronounce pardon. "Your sins are forgiven; go in peace."

Some weeks later, she again was shown into my room. Confidently she walked toward me with a smile on her face, her right hand extended for hand clasp. In a glad voice she said, "Look, my arm is healed."

Jesus knew all about the power of guilt to hold the human spirit, even the body, in bondage. A group of friends once brought a paralyzed man, lying on his bed, to Jesus. At once, Jesus saw there was a need deeper than the stricken limbs. So, startling all within hearing distance, he said, "Your sins are forgiven."

Having forgiven sin, Jesus pushed on from cause to effect. Next he commanded, "Take up your bed and walk." And the paralyzed man walked.

Guilt! How many are kept in a prison house with walls a mile high because of unforgiven sin. Jesus, for many of us, must be a liberator from guilt.

Jesus, in giving people release, used many of the insights we now find in psychiatry. Without the jargon of modern psychiatric practice, he set men and women free.

With a sure touch Jesus was able to reach toward the center of human personality and offer forgiveness and freedom.

If we could only see the true relationship between psychiatry and Jesus, we would witness many a miracle of deliverance. By psychiatry and religion working hand-in-hand, many could go free. Psychiatry provides the techniques, the religion of Jesus the power, for liberation.

How do psychiatry and the religion of Jesus working together bring deliverance? What is the relation of psychiatry to faith? How do the psychiatrist's couch and the cross of Jesus work together for release and healing? Religious faith and psychiatry both try to uncover the depths of human personality, both try to develop a saving self-knowledge.

Psychiatry rests on several fundamental claims. It believes that human attitudes and behavior are often driven by deep and hidden desires and motives. These lie beyond conscious understanding. Psychiatry aims to bring buried facts of personality to the surface. By drawing them to consciousness, inner tension is eased and the healing of broken lives can begin.

The Spirit of God goes deeper than any psychiatrist. This is the claim of the noble Psalm 139.

> O Lord, thou hast searched me and known me . . .
> and art acquainted with all my ways. . . .
> Search me, O God, and know my heart!
> Try me . . .
> And see if there be any wicked way in me.

Jesus, looking forward, promised that the ministry of the Holy Spirit would be profound. When the Counselor comes, said Jesus, "He will convince the world concerning sin and righteousness and judgment."

The cross of Jesus possesses power for smashing complacency, for reaching to the depths of personality and bringing hidden facts to light. Self-knowledge, the uncovering of the truth about one's life, is the beginning of deliverance.

Psychiatry and the Christian faith both recognize the need for love and the necessity for a sense of acceptance to develop if lives are to be made whole. Love breaks down prison walls.

Modern psychiatry has learned that lovelessness lies behind the disharmony of many a life. Childhood rejection, isolation, loneliness, bitterness, hatred devastate and destroy human personality. Hence recovery of mental and emotional balance depends often on the discovery of love.

Love is what the Christian faith is all about. Jesus came into the world to declare, to reveal, the love of God. "God so loved the world that he gave his only Son." It was a man who had seen Jesus, living and dying, who said, "God is love."

The love of God is the greatest therapy-force in the world. We sometimes talk about the power of the Cross on which Jesus died. The power is not in the Cross; it is in the love of God, the forgiving, caring Spirit of Jesus, who died on that Cross.

This power of love can be seen in an early incident in the life of the Quaker leader Rufus Jones. When he was a boy, he was given a task on the farm one day while his parents went out. However, some friends arrived and asked him to go fishing.

It was after dark before he returned home to find his mother waiting for him, and something happened which the boy was never to forget.

"Then a miracle happened," writes Rufus Jones. "My

mother put me in a chair, kneeled down, put her hands on me, and told God all about me. 'O God,' she prayed, 'take this boy of mine and make him the boy and man he is divinely designed to be.' Then she bent over me and kissed me and went out and left me alone with God."

God in Jesus did just this for us all. When we do something far more serious than disobeying the direction of a parent, when we rebel against God's purposes, bringing suffering to ourselves and to others, his forgiveness is there. Through the offering of his love, he changes our lives.

There are two kinds of guilt, according to the Swiss psychiatrist, Paul Tournier. In his book *Guilt and Grace*, he distinguishes between what he calls false guilt and true guilt: " 'False guilt' is that which comes as a result of the judgments and suggestions of men. 'True guilt' is that which results from Divine judgment."

There is a kind of guilt which psychiatric techniques can remove. I suggest that it falls within the category Tournier defines as false guilt. Childhood memories of naughtiness, anxiety over violation of social customs, offenses against class or society's moral code create guilt. For these, the psychiatrist's couch, the therapy of wise human counseling may be enough.

What about real guilt, deep guilt? There are some actions which go far beyond offending against man's standards; they break God's laws. When this happens, deep guilt is involved, a guilt which can shatter personality and is beyond the power of man to reach.

Murder produces deep guilt. Adultery involves deep guilt. Dishonesty creates deep guilt. Cruelty makes deep guilt.

As David discovered, God is involved in deep guilt. When David realized he had committed adultery and murder, it was not only of his human victims he thought. Brokenly he cried, "Have mercy on me, O God, . . . against thee, thee only have I sinned, and done that which is evil in thy sight."

When God becomes involved, when our guilt comes from a response to God, then only God can speak. If we are to be freed from guilt, God must speak his word of pardon.

The cross of Jesus is God's answer to the guilt-laden life. In the crucifixion of Jesus, we see God, not treating sin lightly, but finding a way of dealing with it. In the cross of Jesus, God pays a price for the forgiveness he offers. He reveals the moment can come when judgment gives place to mercy. From the Cross comes the great message, "There is therefore no condemnation to those who are in Christ Jesus."

Since Jesus died on a hill beyond Jerusalem, millions have found an answer to deep guilt. There we learn there is no such thing as an unpardonable sin. There is no sin so evil that God cannot cover it with his love. There is no sin repeated so often that he cannot endure and pardon. There is no sin so hurtful, destructive to others that the love of God cannot absorb. A simple hymn expresses what can happen.

> At the cross, at the cross where I first saw the light,
> And the burden of my heart rolled away,
> It was there by faith I received my sight,
> And now I am happy all the day.

There is something more that must be found if we are really to escape from guilt. It is to discover something to put in the place of the attitude or actions which have produced the guilt. It is the need to find a new pattern for living.

In a way, pardon for guilt is negative. It deals with the past. But the future beckons. There is a double healing that is needed. Something, someone must come into our lives to strengthen and remake them.

The aim of psychiatry and religion in this area is the same. It is to set people free to become their true selves. It is to recreate weak, divided, broken lives.

A new design for living must be found. From where shall it come? Out of the psychiatrist's own life? Yet, he too is but a frail human being. Out of our society? But society itself is confused and broken. Psychiatry can and does unravel many a tangled life. Whence comes the pattern for a reweaving of attitude and emotion?

The life-style of Jesus of Nazareth provides the pattern for a redesigned life. In him is revealed the way to live. In the calmness and steadfastness of his faith, in the peace and joy of his Spirit, in the selflessness and concern he showed in human relationships, we see life as it was meant to be lived. Here is the kind of life to be sought on the other side of forgiven guilt.

A new power for living is needed. It is one thing to glimpse what may be, it is another to move in strength to achieve it. Hence, after pardon must come power.

> Be of sin the double cure
> Save from wrath and make me pure.

Again psychiatry must look beyond itself. Power cannot come from within the personality of the one forgiven. Failure in the past has arisen because of helplessness under temptation. There is no hidden resource of moral power within us to which we can turn.

It is not enough for a patient to become dependent on his doctor. No worthy doctor builds up personal dependence. Anyway, this never works for the simple reason the psychiatrist cannot always be available.

There is a source of power. It is found in the God who already has by his forgiving grace taken guilt away. From him comes power for living a new life, a life liberated from guilt.

David Stafford-Clark, the noted psychiatrist, gives a moving testimony of the discovery he has made. He points the way for us all. "Where then can a man turn? If full self-awareness and self-realisation are not by themselves enough, what is? As a psychiatrist I know of no answer to the question; as a man I can only say with all humility that I believe in God."

7. BORN FREE—STAY FREE

"Man is born free, yet everywhere is in chains" was a rallying cry of the French Revolution. Since that time, a vast world movement to throw off the shackles of poverty, racism, and political oppression has developed, achieving many a victory. However, at the same time, mankind has been forging for itself a new prison house; it is the inner jail of compulsive habits. Millions today live under as sad and miserable a bondage as any outer social or political tyranny. As a result, it is still true, "Man is born free, yet everywhere is in chains."

Man is born free. Is he? What is the truth concerning the power of heredity in such issues as alcoholism and homosexuality? Howard J. Clinebell, in his book *Understanding and Counselling the Alcoholic*, says, "The transmission of alcoholism from parents to child would seem to be a question of social rather than biological heredity."

Dr. Daniel Capon, in *Toward an Understanding of Homosexuality*, says on homosexuality, "There seems to be little, if any, evidence for heredity, constitutional or chemical factors in the genesis of homosexuality. Homosexuality is not born, it is made, and with difficulty at that."

The Christian faith declares man is born free. The Bible claims that man is made in the image of God, and God is free. The bondage under which man moves comes from his sin, his rebellion against God. The coming of Christ as Deliverer is based on the assumption that a lost freedom can be restored. So a Paul can say: "You were called to freedom, brethren; only do not use your freedom as an opportunity for the flesh" (Gal. 5:13).

Man is everywhere in chains. Compulsive habits hold millions of people in bondage. There are six million alcoholics in America, and to this figure can be added several million more with severe drinking problems. Karl Menninger says, "The alcoholics in the United States constitute our largest single mental health problem." In Australia there are 330,000 alcoholics. In France the number of alcoholics is above one million. Dr. Etienne May reported to the French Economic Council that in France one in every three drinks himself to death.

In Sydney, Australia, it is estimated that there are thirty thousand gambling addicts in bondage to legalized poker machines. There are an estimated seven million compulsive gamblers in the United States. Nicotine, particularly through cigarettes, is a worldwide way of life. In America, eighty million people are dependent on nicotine, even though they know it causes cancer, hypertension, and coronary disease.

Drugs have become a central issue in today's world. In certain areas, such as New York, the younger, under-twenty-five group has drugs as a problem, while older people face the issue of alcoholism. In America true narcotics like heroin, morphine, and cocaine have in their grip from sixty thousand to one-hundred thousand people. Milder drugs and pills and tablets have reached epidemic proportions. The tablet way of life is established with pills to induce sleep, to keep people awake, to stop pregnancy, to encourage pregnancy, to prevent seasickness, to ease anxiety, to aid concentration, to ease headaches and pains. As Wallace Hamilton says vividly, "Sixty million sleeping pills a day—that's how some Americans are saying their prayers at night."

If there is any title which is typical of Jesus it is the Deliverer. At the time of his birth, Zechariah and Simeon said a deliverer of victorious power had come. In his first message at Nazareth, Jesus said he had come to proclaim deliverance to the captive. During the full length of his public life, Jesus went about setting men and women free. This has been his wonderful ministry ever since. Jesus is the Liberator.

God's purpose for all people is inner personal freedom of spirit. Jesus came to make this purpose come true. In a full and glad acceptance of the Spirit of God in our lives we find our destiny.

Behind today's compulsive habits lies the search for freedom. Howard Clinebell says that one does not fully understand alcohol as a problem until one sees it as a solution. This principle can be applied to every form of compulsion. Alcoholism has a history, drug-taking has a background, gambling has motives which rise deep within personality, sexuality is often a way of escape from a life which has become unbearable. All begin as a struggle to be free, as a groping after self-transcendence. Drugs, in other words, are a God-substitute.

What could be more natural than to imagine in a tablet age, that by chemical change a new life can be achieved? With pills available for everything, why should not drugs be used to give a desirable experience, or, in a cheap and easy way, to open the gates of freedom for the struggling soul?

Countless illustrations could be found of persons who have turned to drugs to escape from inner conflict and disappointment. Take the story of the English man of letters, Charles Lamb. In his latter years, he became an alcoholic because, for him, alcohol had become a way of escape. He was a man with a deep inferiority complex, and when he turned to alcohol his stammer was forgotten. His tongue-tied mind and lips were loosened, and he rose above his crippling sense of inferiority. The price he eventually paid was to become captive in a prison far worse than inferiority—alcoholism.

Men have always turned to the changes which chemical forces can produce to discover something that is akin to religious joy, to the God-experience. Thousands of years ago, Mexicans discovered the power of peyote cactus buttons which grew in their part of the country. When they were swallowed, they gave a sense of oneness with the Maker of the universe and spiritual elevation of an intense kind. They actually called these peyote buttons "God's flesh." Divine ecstasy, to bathe in an experience of transcendence, to feel at home at last in a hostile godless universe, is an experience for which all yearn. To take peyote buttons or LSD, to smoke a marijuana cigarette, or to trust some derivative of opium is almost commonplace under the limitation and frustrations of so many today. People who are morally and spiritually impoverished turn to gambling or alcohol, drugs or sex, in search for an elation of spirit, and so become trapped in an addiction.

If this analysis is correct, the absence of real religion

in many lives today makes inevitable the turning of men and women to God-substitutes. A real conquest of compulsions that are destroying human personalities can only come by finding God. An experience of God in Christ is the answer. It may sound an over-simplification to say it, but the answer to life's compulsions is God himself. Jesus is the Liberator.

Remaining free from life's inner compulsions involves seeing the real way to live, which is to give and not to take, to place the center of life's interest beyond the self, not within the self. The answer is to accept the words of Jesus: "For whoever would save his life will lose it, and whoever loses his life for my sake will find it" (Matt. 16:25).

Behind the compulsive habits of many lives is a distinct philosophy of life. It is the belief that life's satisfactions are found through stimulation of the senses, by inner excitement, by exploring the world of the self. There is one common factor behind the four major compulsions of alcohol, drugs, gambling, and sexuality. It is that pleasurable sensations are all-important and should be sought by any means available. This common factor means that all who turn in this way are completely self-centered. Life is sensation. Life means satisfying the self. Real living is enjoyable personal experience.

The search for satisfaction by the stimulation of the body is grasping the present at the expense of the future. There is only one end to this road. It is to demand more and more artificial stimulation, to turn from soft to hard drugs, to explore ever more abnormal experiences in sexual relationships. As Oscar Wilde honestly confessed about his own deepening personal crisis, which in the end ruined him, "I let myself be lured into long spells of senseless and sensual practices. Tired of being on the heights, I deliberately held to the depths in search of new sensations."

Here is a recipe for compulsion. Always, by seeking new ways or multiplying old ways, there is the search for new sensations. So the bondage tightens and freedom disappears. Malcolm Muggeridge, the British publicist, sums it up this way, "There is a way of deliverance, after all, but it lies in the exactly opposite direction—out of the ego, not into it, heads lifted up from the trough, instead of buried in it."

Into this false world strides Jesus. Jesus took the hard road. In the end, it led him to Calvary. Jesus sought freedom and fulfillment not in personal satisfaction, but in doing the will of God. On the Cross, even amid all his pain, he refused a deadening drug. Remaining alert, he cried, "My God, my God, why hast Thou forsaken me?" Yet through it all he remained free. His enemies destroyed his body, but his spirit went free. From his personal victory he mediates freedom to us. "So if the Son makes you free, you will be free indeed" (John 8:36).

Deliverance from compulsiveness of any kind means becoming part of a new community. Group strength is essential for the life of freedom. This is why the Christian church, with its worship and its fellowship, does more than it knows to make and keep people free.

Among the most important insights of recent years in dealing with the problems of compulsion is the power of therapeutic groups. An accepting fellowship is of the very essence of treatment and recovery. Alcoholics Anonymous and Gamblers Anonymous have both proved the value of this technique. The essence of the recovery group is that it is made up of people grappling with the same problem, who are ready to accept one another and honestly share together the defeats and victories in the struggle against compulsion.

At the Life Line Centre in Sydney, a Gamblers Liberty Group has been operating for years. It is an accepting fellowship made up of gamblers and their wives or husbands. By honesty and friendship and by placing all in a religious context, treatment is given. In a city where gambling is an intense problem, it does not lack for members who seek its aid.

The Gamblers Liberty Group tells many a story of deliverance. Here is one: Two years ago, the manager of an insurance company turned to the Gamblers Liberty Group for aid after many years of gambling. He described himself as the most compulsive bettor in Australia. In two years, he had lost forty thousand dollars in gambling debts. It was this huge loss and the threat of bankruptcy which drove him to seek help through the group. For two years he struggled on with many a setback. Gradually strength seemed to come. Now he tells of two years without gambling. He works eagerly to pass on to others the story of the deliverance that has come to him. He has entered his own local church. Throughout his months of struggle, his wife stood bravely at his side. Each, for two years, has come weekly to the Gamblers Liberty Group. They continue to come, believing they need the strength of the group, and to help others to discover the same victory.

The Christian church itself is the greatest strengthening group of all. The church, with the supreme therapy of worship, stands in every community. It could be the accepting fellowship which gives men and women hope. The Christian church is peculiarly fitted to be an accepting fellowship because at its heart is an accepting God and an accepting gospel. Through it appears for all who will see Jesus, the Liberator.

There is nothing more needed in the church today than exploration into how the newer discoveries of psychiatry and psychology can be related to the insights of the Christian faith. By releasing, through modern techniques in counseling and relationships, the grace of God, freedom can be found.

Perhaps the most successful of all agencies in bringing freedom to people trapped in compulsive habits is Alcoholics Anonymous. In nonreligious language, it has found a way of communicating the great insights and strength of the Christian faith.

In the twelve steps for recovery, the essence of the Christian gospel is presented. Look at the essential meaning, in terms of Christian insight, of some of the offered steps to release and recovery.

We:

* "Admit we are powerless over alcohol—that our lives have become unmanageable." Here is what the Christian calls repentance.
* "Came to believe that a power greater than ourselves could restore us to sanity." Here is faith.
* "Made a decision to turn our will and our lives over to the care of God as we understood him." Here is daily trust in a living God.
* "Made a searching and fearless moral inventory of ourselves."
* "Admitted to God, to ourselves, and to another human being the exact nature of our wrong." Here is confession.
* "Made a list of all persons we had harmed, and became willing to make amends to them all. . . . Made direct amends to such people wherever possible ex-

cept when to do so would injure them or others." Here is the concept of restitution.

* "Sought through prayer and meditation to improve our conscious contact with God as we understood him, praying only for knowledge of his will for us, and the power to carry that out." Here is the way of daily prayer.
* "Having had a spiritual awakening of the result of these steps, we try to carry this message to alcoholics and practice these principles in all our affairs." Here is service rising out of gratitude.

Some years ago, an interesting yearly custom was observed in a small European country. On a chosen day, the king would ride from one side to the other of his small territory. His route always took him past the two jails of his realm.

The prisoners in the jails were told that, if they could catch a glimpse of the king as he rode by, they could go free. No one, it was said, who looked on the face of the king, could remain a prisoner.

So it was that every prisoner sought to see the king as he passed by. And the promise was kept; if some prisoner was able somehow, from wall or window, to catch a glimpse of the king, for him the prison doors opened. He went free.

"Jesus of Nazareth passes by." To see him, to accept him, to trust him, is to go free. Jesus is the Liberator.

8. REAL SEXUAL LIBERATION

So at last we have sexual freedom. The age of the Pill is here. Sex has been brought into the open to be discussed, depicted in all its intimacies at every movie house and around every magazine stand. The bonds of marriage are being broken. Sex is free, as uninhibited as taking a cup of coffee. A brave new world of sexual liberation has arrived.

Has it? I would have thought that probably in our sex-obsessed society more people are in bondage to sexuality than ever. Pornography is fast fashioning a new prison for the imagination and emotions of millions. If ever men and women cried out to be liberated from sex to love, a love which includes the beauty and delicacy of sex, it is now. Today the need is for a real sexual liberation movement.

Strange how the wheel turns full circle. When the message of Jesus reached Greece and Rome in the first century, it came as a liberation from sex obsession. The earliest Christians showed a purity of thought and action, a tenderness in man-woman relationships which began to cleanse the world.

Now the Christian way is beginning again to appear in its true light as a truly new morality. Around the Christian community today is something which is called the "new morality" in sexual attitudes, but which is hoary with age. It is nothing more than a throwback to some of the crudest moments of the past.

How refreshing are the observations of Jesus: The pure in heart shall see God, The man who lusts after a woman has committed adultery in his heart. How liberating is the quiet word of Jesus to a woman who was a victim of the sexuality of her time, "Neither do I condemn you; go, and do not sin again."

The new, liberating sexual morality of Jesus is built on the fact that God's moral law is established. There is something given, unchanging. It is the pattern of the moral universe.

The universe is not morally neutral. It is made in a certain way. As Anderson Scott puts it: "The universe consists of protons, electrons, radiation and goodness." Goodness—a moral quality—is built into the very nature of society and of the world.

The structure of this moral universe is revealed most clearly in the Ten Commandments and Christ's Sermon on the Mount. As we discover this pattern and live by it, so we live; as we repudiate it so we perish in the end.

If, for example, we reject the First Commandment and worship more than one God, we become cursed with divided loyalties and a broken selfhood.

If we despise the fourth Commandment and try to work seven days a week, we invite a nervous collapse, shallowness of soul, and even bodily illness, such as a coronary occlusion.

If we defy the Sixth Commandment and commit adultery, the results are smashed homes, injured little children, and unpredictable forces released into future relationships.

Long ago, Adam and Eve repudiated the fact that there was an eternal right as revealed to them. They tried to write their own rules and lost Paradise. There is only one new, yet old, morality; it formed initially in the mind and purpose of God. So we can sing, "That's the way God planned it" and "meant it to be."

If we are to be sexually liberated we must find God's plan for us as men and women and seek to fulfill it. Only then can we expect to discover the happiness, the fulfillment we so eagerly are seeking.

There is a clear principle for sex relationships given early in the Bible. The biblical view of sex is reflected in the use of the word "knew" for sexual intercourse. In Genesis it says, "Now Adam knew Eve his wife, and she conceived and bore Cain."

Sex, in other words, involves two persons knowing each other. It is the climax of a growing awareness, a deepening knowledge. Sex cannot be held in isolation, it is not just a thing, it is meant to be part of a very wide mutual understanding of each other.

Any husband and wife, deeply in love, will tell that sex satisfies most fully as a climax experience following a much wider and deeper sharing. Only as it takes its place in this larger act of self-giving, does it find its true meaning and happiness.

Now if this is the principle, how are we to judge some of the most accepted practices of current society?

Prostitution is completely unacceptable. There can be no real mutual knowledge or self-giving. As William Barclay puts it: "Prostitution is a relationship in which one of the partners can be purchased as a thing is purchased and discarded as a thing is discarded, where there is no respect for personality."

Casual sex is likewise isolated sex, without the context of an adequately shared life. So often it is on a mean and squalid basis, on the exploitation of one person by another.

In the film *Room at the Top* a girl is being coerced into giving herself to the man at her side.

"I love you. I would do anything for you," she says.

"Sure," he replies brutally, "you would do anything except the one thing any girl would do for the man she loves."

That is not love. It is emotional blackmail.

Premarital sex lacks a sufficient basis for bodily self-giving. It is often argued: Here are two people going steady; they will soon be married; why wait? Many going steady today are unsteady in a month's time, and in another month are separated. Before marriage there is no abiding relationship; there is not as yet a sufficient sharing of life together for sex to take its natural place as God meant it to be.

John Robinson has a wise word to offer, arguing that any young man must ask himself: "How much do you love her? If he doesn't, or doesn't very deeply, then his [sex] action is immoral; or, if he does he will respect her far too much to use her or take liberties with her. Chastity is the expression of caring—of caring enough."

Sex, of course, within marriage, can likewise be immoral. When the sex act is not part of a wider relationship of love, when it becomes an isolated thing—as at times it does in most marriages—it loses its beauty. When either a husband or wife deliberately uses the other for self-gratification without thought for the mood and feelings of the marriage partner, it breaks the laws of love.

Only in the full and final self-giving of marriage does sex find its true fulfillment. As there are built up memories of a shared past, as there is a shared present in the privacy and trust of living together, as there is the prospect of a shared future with hopes and dreams intertwined, then—and only then—does sex bloom in its full loveliness.

We catch a glimpse of the full knowledge which forms the true context of a sexual relationship in the way Dinah Morris speaks of her man in the novel *Adam Bede.* "Adam," she says, "it is but a divided life I live without you. What greater thing is there for two human souls than to be joined together for life: to strengthen each other in toil, to rest on each other in all sorrow, to minister to each other in all pain, to be with each other in silent, unspeakable memories at the last parting."

If we are to be sexually liberated, we must find a power to overcome the sex pressures of this increasingly permissive age. This power will only come as we understand clearly the issues involved and seek the strength which flows from the purity, the holiness of God.

What a strange and disturbing development is the world growth of pornography. For after all what is pornography but the organization of lust for profit on a vast scale. I see it as a threat to mankind as serious as the growing traffic in hard drugs. Moral attitudes and standards profoundly affect the life of all people. Canon Raven is right when he says: "Sex standards and civilisation rise and fall together."

Pornography stains the imagination and corrupts the

delicate relationships between men and women. There can be only one result of the exploitation of sex in entertainment. It will be a demand for more corrupt sex to satisfy depraved tastes.

There are misguided people who try to say pornography has no effect on human life and action. Obviously, if bad literature has no bad influence on the human mind, good literature has no good influence on people. Yet our whole system of education and cultural life is built on the assumption that the mind can be elevated by noble ideas expressed in words, art, music. We cannot have it both ways.

Some go even farther and claim pornography has a therapeutic value, is actually good for us. If it is better to soak the mind with sex, to stain the soul with uncontrolled fantasy than to think about "whatever is just, whatever is pure, whatever is lovely, whatever is gracious" —to quote St. Paul—then life has become a grotesque parody of everything we had thought it was supposed to mean.

How personally can you and I stand up to the morally polluted atmosphere being created constantly by the morally permissive society? We can do it only by seeking to live within the purity and holiness of God. "Purity is positive, not negative," said the great Archbishop Temple. "It is spiritual not physical. It is the passionate aspiration toward the holiness of God."

Spend time with Jesus, learning about him, thinking about him. To follow him in thought and imagination along the roads of Palestine, to listen to his voice by the Galilean lake, to drink in of his Spirit is to tap power for purity. It is by resting mind and heart in the presence of Jesus we find strength.

In the tainted atmosphere of today's sex-saturated society, I find myself wanting to sing a simple hymn, and to try and live by it:

> Let the beauty of Jesus be seen in me,
> All His wonderful passion and purity;
> O Thou Spirit divine,
> All my nature refine,
> Till the beauty of Jesus is seen in me.

9. OBEYING ONLY GOD

In a pleasant house set in the spacious grounds of one of Australia's historic church colleges, a man brooded over the state of the nation and of the world. Sick at heart, he watched the endless, senseless killing of Vietnam, the war nobody wanted, and yet nobody seemed able to stop. In particular, he saw what Australia's compulsory national service was doing to young men of sensitivity and conscience.

At last, unable to silence his own questionings any longer, he felt he must give a cry of despair and protest. Taking a pen, consulting with nobody, he wrote a letter to the press: "I am loath indeed to be forced publicly to advocate nonviolent civil disobedience. As an ex-Serviceman, a private citizen, a man of law and Law, I publicly encourage twenty-year-olds, in good conscience and in loyalty to God rather than Caesar, to defy the National Service Act."

This man, within three days, was dismissed forthwith by the council of the college as headmaster. The ensuing upheaval, the great national debate it provoked, have become part of recent Australian history. The issue was finally resolved by the Methodist Church in New South Wales, which carries ultimate responsibility for the school. The church reversed the school council's decision and reinstated the headmaster. It was but a temporary respite, for within a few weeks, believing his position at the school to be untenable, he resigned.

The dramatic action of this Christian headmaster raises basic issues relating to conscience, the law, and God. It forced countless people to face the fact that sooner or later any one of us, becoming liberated from fear of public opinion, of possible consequences, could be forced to say: God is my conscience.

There is an incident in the book of Acts which sharply focuses the whole question. Peter and the apostles, preaching in Jerusalem, were brought before the Jewish officials, of the Sanhedrin, and ordered to be silent in the streets, not mentioning the name of Jesus. The rule of the court was immediately defied, and Peter and his friends were dragged a second time before the authorities. The high priest and his council charged them not to teach in the name of Jesus. This brought from the lips of Peter a cry which ever since has been ringing through the minds of men and the years of history: "We must obey God rather than men."

God made man as a free, responsible being. Man is being truly human when he claims his independence and his freedom.

What is it that separates man from the animals? One answer is conscience. A flock of sheep, a herd of cows, are not concerned beyond themselves, they are untouched by compassion, there are no moments when there is a stirring of conscience.

Only men can stand back and see, knowing the difference between right and wrong. Viktor Frankl puts it this way, "Conscience is the voice of transcendence; man intercepts the voice but does not originate it." Conscience is the crowning glory of man.

Mankind has gradually given a preeminent place to conscience. The Nuremberg trials of war criminals following World War II take their place in history because the transcendence of conscience as a principle was recognized. The Nuremberg trials declared that, no matter how high may be the authority or position of a man over his fellows, no man moves beyond responsibility for his actions. No matter how lowly the human being may be to whom orders may come, he cannot be absolved from personal responsibility for his actions. Conscience is given a supreme place in human affairs, and no extenuating circumstances absolve a man from being true to conscience.

By common consent some of the noblest moments of history have been recorded when men and women have taken their stand on grounds of conscience. Socrates is an illustration plucked from the many who, over the centuries, have sacrificed all for conscience' sake.

In Athens in the fourth century before Christ, a placard appeared in the city streets detailing charges against Socrates: Socrates is guilty of crime; first, in not believing in the gods the city believes in; second, in introducing new gods; third, in corrupting the youth of Athens. The penalty is death. Socrates was tried before five hundred citizens, and by a majority of sixty was condemned to death.

The startling similarity between the charges made by the council of the Sydney school against a headmaster, and the complaint against Socrates is obvious. The council virtually said the headmaster did not believe in our gods of school and state, he was a corrupter of youth, having no right to suggest disobedience to the law of the state.

One comment becomes inevitable. Has there been no advance in tolerance and justice since the year 399 B.C.? Man at his noblest and best has many times been ready to say: "Come what may, God is my conscience. We must obey God rather than men."

The Christian faith upholds the rule of law. The Bible teaches that God orders human life through governing authorities. Law, to restrain evil and encourage the good, lies within the purpose of God.

There are four basic passages in the Bible which declare the support of the Christian faith for the rule of law and its objection to anarchy. Jesus, in Matthew 22: 21, utters his famous words: "Render therefore to Caesar the things that are Caesar's, and to God the things that are God's." Jesus here, in relation to the payment of taxes, undoubtedly endorses the laws of Caesar. However, Jesus does not attempt to draw the line between what are the things of Caesar and the things of God. He declares a principle and leaves us to apply it. There is little doubt, however, that in the mind of Jesus, the things of God take precedence over the things of Caesar.

In Romans 13:1, Paul discloses his mind in relation to law, and the state: "Let every person be subject to the governing authorities, for there is no authority except from God, and those that exist have been instituted by God." Paul here is reflecting his own experience in relation to Roman Law. At this stage in Christian history magistrates were friendly, and the law stood between Paul and his persecutors. Paul undoubtedly was fearful of anarchy, and pleaded for obedience to the law.

In I Peter 2:13, the view of Paul is echoed. "Be subject

for the Lord's sake to every human institution. . . . Live as free men, yet without using your freedom as a pretext for evil: . . . Fear God. Honor the Emperor."

By the time the last book of the Bible was written, the Revelation, circumstances had changed. Nero was Caesar, and bitter persecution had broken over the church. Now the state was not a friend but an enemy. Rome made war on the saints. The state was called the "mother of harlots and of earth's abominations . . . drunk with the blood of the martyrs of Jesus." Now the state had become demonic, an instrument not of God, but the devil.

Since the first century, relationships have always been uneasy between the church and the state. Undoubtedly, a strong stream of influence within Christian thinking and practice has demanded obedience to the law. There has been a great fear of anarchy. God has been seen as permitting sovereigns and elected rulers to exercise authority. Kings and governors are his instruments, and must be obeyed.

The tremendous respect and authority granted to lawmakers in the Bible places an immense responsibility on their shoulders. This responsibility has often been treated lightly or abused, and great evil has resulted.

Let me say bluntly that the federal government of Australia, during the unhappy involvement in the Vietnamese war, unworthily exercised its responsibility in lawmaking. It was not young people with a conscience who threatened the rule of law. It was the government itself which brought the law into disrepute in Australia. The National Service Act, which imposed military conscription upon a small number of nineteen-year-old Australians balloted by lot, was a bad law.

It is the task of governments to limit, as far as possible,

laws which result in civil disobedience. Before the National Service Act was rescinded, many Australians were forced to defy the state, saying: God is my conscience. I must serve God rather than men.

God's law comes first, taking precedence over man's law. This is the unmistakable teaching of the Bible. We must serve God rather than men.

The Bible and history are full of the stories of men and women who have been obedient to God's law, at the same time defying man's law. Daniel openly defied the law of the realm. Three young Jews, when Nebuchadnezzar was king, did the same. Peter and the apostles, in the first century, appealed to a moral authority higher than man-made laws. To name Sir Thomas More, Pastor Niemoller, Martin Luther King, Jr., is to mention but three of many who, in the past, have risked all in defiance of unjust laws, claiming God was their conscience.

A man who breaks an unjust law for conscience' sake does not destroy the rule of law, but honors it. To equate a criminal's breaking the law from underneath with a man who challenges a law from above for selfless, conscientious reasons is absurd. A wise society, far from crushing a responsible man who speaks out with integrity against a law he believes to be unjust, should listen when he says, "God is my conscience."

Freedom of thought is empty unless it becomes freedom to express thought. Intimidation by threatening the loss of job and name, and interference with career, is the weapon democratic societies use to achieve conformity. It must be resisted to the utmost.

Law cannot be static lest soon it become unjust law. Law is brought under scrutiny by citizens who challenge it in the name of a higher, divine law. Society desperately needs men who are prepared to make personal sacrifices in an effort to advance human justice. When society destroys or silences such men, it is repudiating man at his most godlike moment.

An incident which comes from the early history of the Salvation Army in India graphically paints the picture. When Commissioner Tucker, of the Salvation Army, arrived in India he began to hold public meetings and processions. The British Viceroy of India, Sir James Soutar, called Commissioner Tucker to him and issued instructions that no open-air meetings or marches were to be held. The Salvation Army, for conscientious reasons, decided it must defy the governor.

The night came when the Salvation Army, with its bands playing, moved through the streets of the city. At an intersection, there were lined up hundreds of policemen and soldiers to block their progress. An officer stepped forward and, with uplifted sword, shouted, "In the name of Her Majesty, Queen of England, and Queen Empress of India, I order you to disperse."

Commissioner Tucker stepped from the ranks of his marchers and, with hand upraised, replied, "In the name of His Majesty, the King of Kings, and Lord of Lords, I command you to stand aside."

They stood aside, and the Salvation Army marched on.

That incident almost wraps it up. The rule of law must be upheld, yes, but in the last analysis human law must stand under the judgment of divine law. There will always be, there must always be, if true freedom is to endure, men who will say, "God is my conscience. I must serve God rather than men."

10. THE ANSWER TO VIOLENCE

One morning in 1972, just before dawn, there erupted into the Olympic village at Munich the suppressed violence of today's world. In a few terrible hours, the world saw, starkly expressed, the trust in violence which is staining the earth with blood and sorrow.

At Munich, three forms of violence came to focus. There was the violence of desperate men who, without compassion, shot a group of Israeli athletes to death. There was in the background the long callous violence of Israel and the great powers, which since 1948 have deprived the Arabs of land and justice. There was the violence of the state, of the German police, who, by trying to match force with force, contributed to the athletes' death. In a single incident, there surfaced the violence of revolution, the violence inherent in suffering and injustice, and the violence of law and order of the state.

Civilized living is threatened by mankind's cult of violence. It is everywhere. Humanity seems to stagger from one ugly outbreak of violence to the next—from Vietnam to Ireland, from hijacked planes to Munich Olympic murders, from Mafia-madness to letter-bombs.

Jesus was no stranger to violence. This is clear. As a boy, as he grew to manhood, Roman ruthlessness must have confronted him in the crosses raised against the sky on which some Jewish patriot died. The whole Zealot movement—akin to the modern guerilla fighters—must have challenged his thinking.

In carrying out his God-given ministry, Jesus contemplated the use of violence. This is made clear in his temptations in the wilderness near Jericho. Bluntly his answer was, "Begone, Satan." Out of a lifetime of grappling with the issue, one blinding sentence escaped his lips just before his arrest and crucifixion: "All who take the sword will perish by the sword."

What is the answer of Jesus to violence? How does he liberate us from bondage to violence? How?

Jesus is the Liberator from violence by investing human life with sacredness and worth. Through his birth, life, and death, especially by his death on the Cross, he places his hallowing hand on all human existence, on every human being, on your life and mine.

Violence, after all, represents the forceful invasion of one person by another person. Psychological or physical torture, the using of hostages, as in plane hijacks, are heinous acts of coercion. To put someone to death is the final denial of the worth of a unique, irreplaceable life, a life, which the Bible claims, is made in the image of God.

Where does violence come from? It arises directly from the mind and soul of man. Therefore, it is within the human mind where it begins that it must be faced and overcome.

One of the strangest developments in modern society is

of us and the most affluent. Millions today need to be liberated from slavery to things.

Jesus came to set us free from love of money, from the domination of things. How does he do it? By what means does he bring release to our spirits from slavery to things?

A strong belief in the goodness and providence of God is the beginning of freedom. This is the message of Jesus: Put away anxious thoughts about food and drink to keep you alive and clothes to cover your body. Consider how the lilies grow in the field. If God clothes the grass in the fields, will he not all the more clothe you. How little faith you have.

What is Jesus saying to us? Why do we worry so much over things, over money, over possessions? After all, our heavenly Father knows our need and he cares for us.

God does this in a big way. Some time ago, a strange blackness descended over London in the middle of the afternoon. It was caused by some combination of atmospheric conditions which held the city's smog near to the earth. So all was black. The birds went to roost. The people panicked, some thinking it was the end of the world. Some bowed and prayed in the streets. Some shouted in their consternation. Then, in ten minutes it was gone.

I wonder if it ever grips our minds why it is never dark in the middle of the afternoon? It is because of the constancy, the steadfastness, of God's providential care.

Think of the way his laws operate. A little boy said to his mother, "I am going out to play ball with God."

And she asked, "What do you mean, son?"

He said: "Oh, I throw the ball at God and he throws it back at me." Gravity! What about describing gravity as the way God holds his world together? Now we know God's laws run right to the moon.

Similarly, God's general providence operates within our own lives. This is what many who have walked a long time with Jesus have discovered—he never lets us down. Always under the most desperate circumstances, he has found some way of providing for us.

Malcolm Muggeridge is a rather cynical and typical man of his age, but he admits to being greatly influenced by Mother Theresa, that wonderful Roman Catholic nun who is at work amid the dying and the distressed of Calcutta. In his rather lovely book *Something Beautiful for God*, Muggeridge tells how one day he went into the chapel where Mother Theresa and her sisters were praying. He was amazed to hear the detailed nature of their prayers. They were requesting from God the tiniest things needed in their work among the people of the streets. At first, he was offended, but then he said, "Those of us who cannot participate are not so much more sophisticated as less gifted with faith. If God cares to array the lilies of the field so splendidly, then assuredly Mother Theresa is right in believing He cares about her and the sisters' tiniest necessities."

If we could only lift up our minds to the God who knows us one by one, who holds us in the hollow of his hand, who will never finally let us be dashed and destroyed, we would be likewise set free from material anxiety. If we could find the kind of trust that Mother Theresa has, we would escape the bondage of things.

We would be set free from slavery to things if we could really get our values straight, if we really could put people before profits and property.

What is the real tragedy in the story about the people who lived in the land of the Gerasenes? They put possessions before the miracle of a man made sane. Something wonderful had happened; Jesus had landed on their shore.

They knew that demented, pathetic figure who was always haunting the cemetery. Now, because Jesus had come, he was sane, he was clothed, and he was in his right mind. However, they scarcely noticed the man made whole. They had no rejoicing because Jesus had brought deliverance to a demented man.

All they could see were the empty fields. Their pigs were gone. Their pigs were gone. They would rather have Jesus leave their coastline than heal other demented men and bring his blessing to the whole community. They put their profits, their money, their possessions before healing for a stricken man or a stricken community.

Here is one way by which we gain deliverance. It is by getting our priorities straight. It is by finding a true set of values.

Wrong values have always perpetuated evil. Slavery persisted in the British Empire and in America far beyond time when public opinion could perhaps have been led to accept change, but vested-interest groups said: The economy will not stand abolition. It will wreck the economy to get rid of slavery.

The same claim was heard when reform was sought in the mines and factories of England by people like Lord Shaftesbury. It was said the nation could not afford to dispense with child and woman labor. The economy will collapse, it was said. Then another voice was heard: "If the British Empire goes down because it no longer bases its economy on the rickety bodies of children and cruelty to women, then let it go down."

The same question of priorities arises today. Here is a mother, with little children, facing the issue of becoming a working mother. Where there is grim necessity, perhaps because of bereavement, of course, a mother goes to work for her children's sake. However, there are many homes today where a mother goes to work too early for her children's sake, and the only reason is a grasping for greater material affluence. If children were put before possessions, the babysitting center would not receive the children. Certainly parents should shrink from turning their children into what in Australia we call latch-key kids, children who have to come home from school and find no one to greet them.

Take another example. If we put people before profits, would we introduce into Australia the American practice of almost endless business hours? Do we need to have shops open all the time? Do we need supermarkets and all manner of shops open on Sundays? To do it is to put profit before worship, gain before opportunities for united family life, accumulating possessions before balanced living. Do we really need to sell cars on Sunday, to open flower shops, and do real estate agents need to trade on Sunday? If we go this way, soon the department stores will agitate to open, then why not factories if more money can be made? To go this way is to be trapped by our hunger for ever greater affluence. In an age when we desperately need, for example, the oasis of a work-free Sunday, we sacrifice a priceless heritage.

How easy it is to migrate to the land of the Gerasenes, to put possessions before Jesus. To do it is to pass under slavery to things. It is to forget the words of Jesus: "What does it profit a man if he gains the whole world and loses or forfeits himself" (Luke 9:25).

To be liberated from slavery to things we must set out to build an economic order which encourages men and women to be truly free.

Long before Karl Marx, the Bible emphasized the power the environment of society has over people. There is a significant sentence back in the book of Exodus. Moses has come before the Jews in Egypt, calling them to seek freedom. They refused to listen to him. The Bible says, "They did not listen to Moses because of their broken spirit and cruel bondage." In other words, the society, the environment under which we live affects our ability to hear and receive the Word of God.

The present economic environment of countries like Australia and America seriously inhibits the ability of people to respond to the Christian gospel. The excessive materialism—the affluence of some, the poverty of others—imprisons the lives of millions.

The great issue emerging in the last quarter of the century is: What kind of economic system do we need? The historic visit of President Nixon to China marked the end of an era, an era when mankind was obsessed with fear of communism and fear of atomic warfare. This era stretched from the rise of Hitler, through the Second World War, the cold war, Vietnam, until now. With the gathering detente of the Western world with Russia and China, the search for a more just economic society now becomes possible.

The blunt fact is the Western world has largely halted in its search for a more just economic order. Especially in North America and in Australia, the pathological fear of communism during the last quarter of a century has frightened people away from economic reform. This fear has thrown a cloak of acceptance over capitalism, which it has no right to wear, and has perpetuated weaknesses and evils which should have been long since overcome.

Within capitalist countries, the evils of the economic system are all too obvious. I would name several. Unemployment should, I believe, be totally unacceptable to the Christian conscience. Any government which accepts or deliberately creates a pool of unemployment is unfit to govern. To load onto a section of the people—and those least able to bear it—the burden of inflation is immoral and unjust. The failure to ensure that the mounting wealth which comes from automation and cybernation flows out to all the people is one of the scandals of our time.

Another serious flaw in the current economic society is that people with money find it relatively easy to make more money. People who have nothing cannot get a start, cannot get their heads up above the mere struggle for existence. In a mass society where millions live in vast cities and where people have nothing but their labor to sell, the current mounting insecurity must be overcome. A Christian society would accept the principle that the first call on the strength of the strong, the first call on the resources of society must be the aid, the defense, the care of the weak. In the light of the principle of the parable of the laborers in the vineyard, the concept of a guaranteed annual wage should almost be axiomatic in our kind of society.

The present economic form of society makes inevitable a continual deepening of a two-nation society. It means the gulf between the poor and the rich will widen. Unless this trend can be halted, the gulf will become ever more serious, sowing endlessly the dread seeds of social conflict and disharmony.

Away beyond the national community is the cry for international economic justice and equality. It is undeniable that today the poor nations grow poorer, the rich nations grow richer. There can be only one end to this disparity—war. Hence there is no greater need than for all the world to set out urgently to fashion a new economic society of equality and justice.

Freedom from tyranny to things depends on our own personal response to Jesus Christ.

Anthony Bloom tells of going to hear a man speak about the hunger of the world and the need of the poverty-stricken. It was an inspiring speech in which this man said he was willing to die for the hungry and the needy. Anthony Bloom spent some time with the speaker afterwards and noticed he was a chain smoker. So he said to him, "I hear that you are willing to die for the hungry and the needy. Why don't you give a packet of cigarettes for them?"

We can talk easily about the system of society, about the evils of our economy. What is the individual way of life of each of us? With what integrity are we living within the system of society?

An old saint in the Middle Ages said: "Alms giving is the answer to avarice." Generous giving is one way of loosening the grip of things.

If money is getting a grip on us, how do we shake ourselves free? Give some of it away. Giving cuts through the bars of the prison-house of things and sets us free. Almsgiving is the answer to avarice.

The generosity of some of the noblest Christians is a mark of their greatness. Take Kagawa, the finest Japanese Christian of the century. One day on a street in Tokyo he met the head of the Y.M.C.A., who poured out a story of financial difficulty. He said he could not carry on the service being attempted for insufficient money. Suddenly Kagawa put his hand in his pocket, pulled out a letter, and handed it to his friend. When he opened it, he discovered it was a check for one thousand dollars which Kagawa had just received for one of his books.

"Oh, you cannot give this away, Dr. Kagawa; you need it so much."

Kagawa replied, "No, I insist that you take it. Why shouldn't I? When your friend is dying, there is only one thing to do, give him your lifeblood."

Well, few of us ever reach that standard, do we? Yet the principle is there, haunting us, challenging us. Part of the answer, in Christian terms, to the tyranny of possessions is giving, giving until it hurts and stops hurting. We give because as Dr. Halford Luccock once said, "We ought to go on giving because the gift that costs is the gift that counts."

Jesus sets us free. Has he set you free, whether you are poor or rich? Has he liberated you from the tyranny of things? It is strange the way in which every road leading to Jesus carries us to the place where we are forced to make a choice. Here it is again in the land of the Gerasenes. People who owned those two thousand pigs had to make a choice. They had to welcome or reject Jesus. Their response was: Leave our shores, and return to the other side of the lake. They made their choice, and lost Jesus.

And you? To all who receive him, Jesus will become the Liberator. There is no other way. To accept Jesus is to discover he sets us free from slavery to things.

13. BECOMING TRULY HUMAN

All over the world people are crying out for a truly human existence. Everywhere youth, adults are searching for identity, worth, freedom, and purpose as human beings.

The world is suffering something far worse than the devaluation of money; it is the devaluation of man. Many factors have contributed to this depreciation of the worth of human life. The population explosion seems to turn people into easily replaceable units. As institutions grow bigger, the people in them shrink in identity.

War has degraded the value of life. To kill a man anywhere, whether it be at the end of a hangman's rope or in an aerial bombing, is to cheapen life everywhere. In this war-drenched century, people have been destroyed by the million.

As a result, today's goals are different. Ideologies are dead. No longer are people stirred by the appeal of capitalism, socialism, or communism. Human values are what matter. People want a society with a human face.

Jesus comes into this kind of world with a peculiar appeal and power. His very coming represents the hand of

God reaching out of the unseen vastness declaring: you matter to me. As Jesus moved along the roads of Palestine, he picked up a life here, there, touching it with significance. A sorrowing widow, a prostitute, a tax-gatherer, a child, a leper, a brigand—all were treated with tenderness and respect.

In the end, Jesus died by crucifixion, through it revealing the range and the depth of his love for individual people. As one who knew the mind of Jesus intimately interpreted that death: Christ loved me and gave himself for me. The litany men and women have sung ever since at the foot of the cross of Jesus has been: Jesus died for me.

Jesus gives significance, meaning, purpose to life. He liberates all who turn to him from all sense of devastating worthlessness. Through him we discover how to become truly human.

Through the coming and the living and the dying of Jesus, we learn that every one of us is of infinite worth in God's sight. This conviction is the beginning of finding a life of dignity and significance.

So much today robs life of its individuality. Through medical science one life seems to merge into another. One man moves around with another man's heart or another man's kidney functioning in his body. As more and more organs become transplantable, perhaps even the brain, we might well ask: Who am I?

The movement from agricultural to industrial, and now from industrial to a technological society, seems to depreciate the lives of people. In the country everybody knows everybody; in the city nobody seems to know anybody. Now more and more lives seem to be at the mercy of a computer.

I recall the tense wait with one of our sons for the

news as to whether he had gained entrance to Sydney University. With a quota system operating, he still had to be admitted, although he had passed all the entrance requirements.

At last, the postman came. The news was bad; our son had missed out. Yet the fact which rankled most was the statement in the letter that the decision had been made by a computer. "To think my life is determined by a machine," he said bitterly.

God, according to Jesus, is not a computer. His love is personal, individual. We are of personal value to him. He sent his Son into the world to prove it. Human life in God's sight is of infinite worth.

I once heard a magnificent speech at United Nations on the Charter of Human Rights by Dr. Charles Malik, the Lebanese Christian Statesman.

Dr. Malik said: "The deepest formulation of the present crisis in human rights is not that these rights have been brutally violated. The real crisis is that man today does not believe that he has natural, inalienable rights. Destitute and desolate, he goes about begging for his rights at the foot of the world.

"Having lost his hold on God, or more accurately, having blinded himself to God's constant hold on him, he seeks for his rights elsewhere in vain. We are witnessing the spectacle of a being having lost his proper being—can there be anything more tragic?"

Jesus came to restore that lost being, those lost rights. It is the love of God which liberates man from his nothingness. Jesus died for you and me.

At times I stand back amazed at the wisdom of God in planning for his creatures. He has not only declared that each life has identity and worth; he has designed life in such a way that we can experience this truth.

This is what I mean: God has created the family. In the family there is a breaking-down of the vastness of the human race into small units where individuals count. There in the family circle our names are known. If we are absent, we are missed. There is one place on earth which is ours, where we are at home.

Even more, God's plan includes the fashioning of small community units. Built on common interests or activities, society is dotted with small associations where people have a recognized place. Greatest of all of these free associations of people is the Christian church.

How necessary are the family, the small association, the church in today's society. Around us is the gathering bigness of mass society. In the huge conglomeration of cities the individual can so easily be lost, crushed.

What an appalling development large high-rise apartments really are. I see them multiplying in all the cities of the world, from Singapore to Sydney, from Moscow to New York, from Rome to Nairobi. Soon most cities will look like Moscow, where there is often scarcely a house in sight.

High-rise apartments look like human filing cabinets, with people pushed into their little places, file upon file. No wonder the suicide rate is highest in these kinds of areas all over the world. There is no identity because there is no community.

It was not meant to be this way. God planned the family. Jesus gave us the community of the church, at once local and universal. By finding again his plan, by stepping into it, we will have our society with a human face.

A real human being is a concerned human being. The

authentic mark of a true man or woman is compassion for others. It is this which, as distinct from the beasts of the field, makes us human.

Jesus was the compassionate man beyond compare. Always he was stopped in his tracks by someone in need. A woman touched him, a soldier pleaded for a sick child, a leper cried out for healing, a wealthy outcast mutely appealed for friendship, a dying thief sought help from the dying Christ—and always his response was there.

In Jesus we learn compassion. From the beginning of the Christian church the influence of Jesus has widened and deepened the concern of people for people. The first great social victory of the Christian cause was the bringing to an end of the practice of child-exposure in the ancient world. It was but the beginning of a long story of Christian compassion. Still it goes on in the social programs of Christians round the world and the great international relief agencies of the World Council of Churches and the Roman Catholic Church. As someone has said, "Christian love means reading statistics with compassion."

I interrupted in the writing of these words to visit a camp for one hundred deprived children from the slum areas of Sydney. They had been taken to a Christian country center on the outskirts of the city named Vision Valley.

The excitement of the children was wonderful to see. They were riding horses and rowing canoes on a small lake. They were climbing trees and racing along hiking trails. They were splashing in the swimming pool. In the evening they gathered in the small Gum Tree Chapel, a place of worship in the bush, and were hushed by the quiet beauty of the place as they were led, perhaps for the first time in their lives, to the God whose Spirit throbs through all things.

However, it was not only the joy of the children which made up a moving experience. It was the satisfaction, the quiet strength, of the team of twenty volunteer leaders who had sacrificed a week of work or holidays to be there. Their humanity was expanded by their service. By expressing compassion they had themselves found truer selves.

Jesus sets us free from a sense of worthlessness by drawing us into the army of the concerned. In caring for others we find ourselves. Through compassion Jesus leads us toward being truly human. Perhaps that is why the poet Whittier could write: "Solution there is none save in the heart of Jesus Christ."

Becoming truly human means coming into a close relationship with God. It is through friendship with God in Jesus that we come to understand our true destiny.

The Bible throughout its pages makes it quite clear we are known by name to God, and that he addresses us by name. In the first story of the Bible we read that the Lord called Adam and said, "Adam, where are you?' "

A man named Moses was shepherding his sheep on a hillside. From a bush aflame perhaps with summer flowering, he heard a voice calling, "Moses, Moses."

In the night, in a room in a temple, a small boy lay sleeping. Something awakened him. A voice was heard saying, "Samuel, Samuel." Presently he learned it was the voice of God.

A zealous Jew, was journeying along a road to Damascus, intent on rooting out a new sect, the followers of Jesus. Suddenly, there was the sense of a Presence: "Saul, Saul, why do you persecute me?"

The essence of the Christian faith is an inner personal experience of God. This experience of being addressed by God, of being in a personal relationship with him is open to us all. Until we enter into this relationship with God we are denying our deepest nature. When we accept it we are being truly human.

In his funeral tribute to Martin Luther King, Jr., Benjamin E. Mays, had a significant passage. "God called to the grandson of a slave and said to him: Martin, speak to America about war and peace, about social justice and racial discrimination, about its obligation to the poor and about nonviolence."

God called, "Martin." There it is in modern times. Because King responded to that call, he became perhaps the greatest human being of the century.

And you? It is in God alone through his Son Jesus Christ that we are liberated to become truly human.

14. THE UNMENTIONABLE FEAR: DEATH

Death today is the unmentionable fear. On most issues we live in a quite frank and open society. In journalism, films, discussions, no subject is barred. Sex, for example, is now paraded in all its intimacies. Everything is out in the open but one subject—the subject of death.

In conversation death is never mentioned. In a city, for example, funerals are hurried, the dead are often pushed away, almost out of a back door. Yet none of us can banish death. It meets us sooner or later; the one fact we know about the future is that everyone of us will die. Though we do not talk about it and never discuss it, in more minds than will admit, there is an unmentionable fear—death.

The Bible, of course, is realistic throughout. It does not balk at any subject. Therefore it has a lot to say about death. The New Testament has an interesting emphasis, particularly in the book of Revelation. It is that there are two deaths, a first death and a second death.

The first death is the biological death. It is the obvious fact of dying. This biological fact of death is as natural as eating and sleeping or a tree falling in the bush. The fact, the biological fact of death is one death, the first death.

The Bible talks about a second death. It is the fear of death. It is the awareness, the anticipation of death. This is the fear that causes neurotic anxiety. Death itself as a biological fact is faced when it comes, and faced, usually in ways that we hardly expect, with courage and with calmness.

The anticipation of it, the second death, the fear of death, is what curses man, and always has. The Bible says we are given a power to conquer the second death.

In writing to the people at Smyrna, under their great threat of persecution, no doubt haunted by the fear of their lives being snuffed out, John the Divine talks about the second death, "He who conquers shall not be hurt by the second death." How then do we look, not so much at the biological fact of death, but at this second death: the fear of death? How do you handle that unmentionable fear?

Death is God's purpose. This is the first thing we can say if we are to conquer the fear of death. Death as God's purpose comes naturally at the end of a life, as the ripeness of life.

Death is very much less fearful as a biological fact than we anticipate. In my experience as a minister I have seen many people die. There are two things that I have discovered, and they are confirmed by the experience of many others. Dying is not a momentary event but a process. You cannot pinpoint it quite as we sometimes imagine. A part of the body dies, yet the rest of the body can live on for a time. Even when the heart stops, the cells of the body can exist for a while without having fresh blood pumped into them. Hence, heart-massage can restore a life seemingly over.

So death is almost like saying goodbye to somebody who is on a ship. As the ship draws out into the harbor you watch those you love getting smaller and smaller as the ship draws away and they wave to you. Death is almost like that as God meant it to be.

The second discovery I have made about death is that it apparently is far less painful and horrifying than we imagine. God in his infinite mercy dulls consciousness; there is a decline in awareness as the end of life comes near. Now even the most terrible malignancy can have pain controlled by the drugs that God has stored in his universe to ease the moment of passing where there is great pain. In his mercy he smooths the pillow, he clears the way. Death is a process, a far less frightening experience than we imagine.

Anthony Bloom suggests that something of the fear of death would be overcome if children were allowed to grow up with a natural awareness of it. As a Russian, coming to live in England, he was shocked that death as a fact of life was kept away from the experience of children.

One day Bloom was called to the home of a friend where a woman had died. He noticed the children of the house were missing. When he explained that in the Russian Orthodox Church children were always allowed to see the dead person, the English people were shocked. The children would be terrified, it was said.

After a discussion in which Bloom pointed out that this was the way to develop a frightened attitude to death, the parents agreed the children could be shown the body of the grandmother they had loved.

The children were taken into the room where the grandmother was lying. For a time they stood in silence, looking. Then one of the children said, "How beautiful granny looks." At that moment, death ceased to be something to be dreaded.

To weave death into our experience is to grow without

the psychological shocks of discovering later something that inevitably all must face. We are meant to be rid of this fear of death, to conquer the second death by facing the facts, by thinking about them, knowing and growing with life and death as God meant them to be.

What are we to say about the early death, the sudden death, the horror of sudden disaster on the roads? All we can say surely is that God did not intend early death.

I do not know how it happened, but I am convinced that early death is bound up in the sin of man. We hear for example today that, of the 1,250 people who died on roads of New South Wales in a recent twelve-month period, 750 had a high alcohol content in the blood samples taken after they were dead. Man in his sinfulness often brings about his own death and the death of his brother and sister. Perhaps sin itself has introduced distortion such as cancer into the human scene. I wonder, for example, how much leukemia is coming from the French atomic tests in the Pacific?

Some time ago, there died in England, at the age of eighty-six, one of the great men of the Methodist Church, Luke Wiseman. His end came on a Sunday night. He had preached in Wesley Chapel in the morning and in another church in the afternoon. Coming home, he had tea, settled into an easy chair to doze, and never awakened.

Luke Wiseman had never in his long life really been ill. He worked, living life vigorously to the end. Then, without pain, without struggle, his heart stopped beating, and he crossed into eternity. That, I believe, is how God meant life and death to be.

"He who conquers shall not be hurt by the second death."

The companionship of God in Christ is an answer to another fear of the second death, the fear of loneliness.

Death is the climax to all the lonely experiences of life. I confess that if there is one aspect of death which frightens me it is the loneliness of it. Utterly alone it seems we have to face death.

Certainly this appears to be true. There is no wide gate through which people pass together along the passage of death. It is an individual turnstile we must enter, each person going on alone. Up until the moment of death, family, friends, doctor are near. As soon as death intervenes, an undertaker is summoned to help. At the moment of death there is no one.

No one? We should not minimize the significance of the power of human companionship right up to the moment of passing. There is often a new identification, a new sympathy from family and friends.

In Elia Kazan's *The Arrangement* an old, rather unpleasant man, with wandering mind, comes to die. At his side is his son Eddie, who had always found his father difficult.

"Then I had it, the sensation," Eddie says. "For the first time in my life I looked at him, not as a problem to deal with, not as an authority to evade and handle, but as a human being. He was one human and I was another. He was my brother."

Away back in the Old Testament, centuries ago, man discovered that God is near at the moment of death. This presence of God is given immortal expression in the twenty-third Psalm: "Even though I walk through the valley of the shadow of death, I will fear no evil; for thou art with me; thy rod and thy staff, they comfort me."

Brian Hession waged a long struggle against cancer.

By determination, by prayer, by faith, he confounded the doctors by living long beyond normal expectations. During the struggle, he spoke of the companionship of Christ, and the sustaining power he gave. Of that experience he wrote, "Above all you have in Christ the greatest fellowship. I am glad Jesus cried: 'My God, why?' Christ's midnight call 'My God, why?' is music to my soul. I know that I am within his fellowship."

So perhaps the loneliness does disappear. Another liberation is given. "He who conquers shall not be hurt by the second death."

Death does not destroy God's purpose for our lives. He overcomes this awful fear that death means the cancellation of what we are doing, that the whole of life loses its meaning and purpose because death has wiped it out.

When the artist Raphael, died at the age of thirty-six, pious people said, "Well, he has painted his greatest masterpieces anyway." But Nietzche, the agnostic, lashed out at them and said, "This life existed once and can never exist again." He felt the hurt of a life that was a broken column.

This was the problem of the people at Smyrna. If you read the story of this place in the first and second centuries, you will find that there was awful suffering and death. Young people were taken and cast to the lions. People were tied to stakes and burned to give light to garden parties. Death stalked through the Christian community at Smyrna. Old man Polycarp, one of the great men of the early church, died in that phase of persecution.

This writer on the Isle of Patmos hears about it and tries to comfort these people by telling them that death does not cancel out God's purpose. If they remain faithful, God will be able to bring His meanings through death. To remain faithful will cause that meaning to be fulfilled.

There is one fact which comes from some of the great lives of history which ended in premature death. So powerful has been the witness which has come through the sacrifice of death that inevitably, the question is asked whether by living they could have achieved more.

Think of Joan of Arc. Possibly through George Bernard Shaw's great play her influence is greater today than ever. As news of the assassination of Abraham Lincoln spread, one commented: "Now he belongs to the ages." President John F. Kennedy died as his leadership was only beginning, yet his influence since his senseless killing has been greater than ever.

When the history books of this century are written, I wonder whether any man will be able to equal the influence of a Martin Luther King. From his all-too-early death have come endless waves of influence. Many in America and beyond have heard the challenge to grapple with racism. People have responded naturally to the call to carry on. As Benjamin Mays said in his funeral message: "Martin Luther King's unfinished work on earth must truly be our own, now."

God does take hold of situations which develop, including the final event of death and, to use a New Testament phrase, does "lead captivity captive." By the marvelous transposition of his power, he brings good out of evil. In other words, death does not finally destroy God's purpose for our lives.

The supreme example of death being absorbed into God's purposes is the crucifixion of Jesus. God took the cross of Jesus and used it to express his love, his salvation for mankind. The Cross bears not man's meaning but God's meaning. God through death carries on his purposes. "He who conquers shall not be hurt by the second death."

Finally, the fear of death is taken away by the resurrection of Jesus. "Because I live," said Jesus, "you shall live also."

Running through the mentality of modern man are two views of death. One is the Greek view. The Greek view is that the body is somewhat evil, certainly of little use, but it is picked up by the soul which resides in it for a while. This soul is immortal and so the spark of immortal life cannot be extinguished by death. Therefore, when the body dies, the soul lives on.

The echo of this type of thinking is in the old song about John Brown, that man in the last century who died trying to liberate the slaves in America. They made a great song about his death in that cause. "John Brown's body lies a mould'ring in the grave, but his soul goes marching on."

That is Greek thinking. There is an immortal something in us that death cannot extinguish. This spark of life which escapes at the moment of death and lives on, this comes from Greek philosophy, not from the Bible.

The other way of thinking about it is the Christian way. A Christian's faith about life after death is not built on the immortality of the soul. It is built on the resurrection of Jesus Christ. The Bible makes it quite clear that a man dies, and he really dies, no part of him living on. There is no spark that cannot be extinguished. He dies.

God brings about another miracle. It was a miracle that gave us life in the first place, and it is a miracle of eternal life that is given to us. We have the sign of what happened in Jesus. He died on that first Good Friday. He died if ever a man died, but on the third day he lived again. So a Christian has his faith built, not on the immortal spark within, but on the miracle of the resurrection of Jesus Christ. Because he lived, we shall live also.

This means that life after death is not a shadowy existence of a disembodied soul flitting about somewhere. There is the resurrection of the whole person, not just a shadowy, immortal something that was secreted within us. The experiences of the years that have been garnered are part of our being now. So in the resurrection that is offered, the whole person lives on. This is our Christian belief in life after death. It is a belief that makes of all death a shadow that cannot hurt.

In the death of the German Christian martyr Dietrich Bonhoeffer, we see expressed the faith which comes from the resurrection of Jesus. A summary court, hurriedly set up, decided that Bonhoeffer must die.

So it was on that Sunday in 1944 the door opened to his cell and a voice said, "Prisoner Bonhoeffer, get ready and come with us." In the language of the concentration camp that meant but one thing, death. To a fellow prisoner he was able to say: "This is the end—for me it is the beginning of life."

Next morning, as recorded by the camp doctor, the end came. "I saw Pastor Bonhoeffer kneeling on the floor praying fervently to his God. At the place of execution, he again said a short prayer and then climbed the steps to the gallows, brave and composed. I have hardly ever seen a man die so entirely submissive to the will of God."

O death, where is your sting? O grave, where is your victory? Jesus liberates us from the unmentionable fear: death.

"He who conquers shall not be hurt by the second death."

15. NO FEAR OF THE FUTURE

All of us have to learn how to handle the future. An unnamed fear is in the mind of many of us, fear of tomorrow.

When we are young we wonder whether we will make it, whether we will succeed in our chosen course of life. In the mid-years we worry about security for the family, whether our children, our teen-age young people will reach maturity without physical accident or moral scarring. As the years lengthen we become anxious as to whether we can hold our jobs, maintain our influence. When we are old we are concerned about possible helplessness or being left all alone in the world. And hovering over all the years is the ultimate anxiety, the fear of death. No wonder Sartre says, "Man is anxiety."

There is only one way to handle the future, only one way to face tomorrow; it is to walk by faith. Nobody, of course, can see round corners, no one can peer into the future. Therefore, somehow we must find a way of walking with a quiet mind, facing each day as it comes, and tomorrow as it looms.

The Bible shows us the way, it is to walk by faith. "Faith," says the writer in Hebrews, "is the substance of things hoped for, the evidence of things not seen." This sounds contradictory. Faith is insubstantial, lacks any body or form, yet this writer says faith has substance. Faith cannot be handled or measured or touched, and yet he says it provides evidence, evidence of the things unseen.

What kind of argument is this? What logic is it that says there is substance and evidence for as vague a thing as faith? And yet that's what the Bible claims. The Bible says there is substance in faith and evidence for things unseen.

God is a personal God, caring for each one of us, concerned about us all. God cares for you, says the Bible. Here is the first substance of faith.

If there is no God or if God is some impersonal force, uninterested in us, none of us can have any real confidence about the future. The agnostic and the atheist have never really caught up with the truth that a godless world means a loveless world. If there is no God now there is obviously no God tomorrow. Life is then without purpose, history is without meaning, personal living is at the mercy of uncaring, impersonal forces.

In the book of Deuteronomy we read how long ago people rejected God and suffered the consequences. The writer describes what happened: "Your life shall hang in doubt before you; night and day, you will be in dread, and have no assurance of your life. In the morning you shall say, 'Would it were evening!' and at evening you shall say, 'Would it were morning!' because of the dread which your heart shall fear, and the sights which your eyes shall see." That is the consequence of banishing God from his world, then and now.

How do we know there is a God, how do we know he cares? The Christian is invited to look back in order to look forward. We go back in history to the place where God acted, where we saw him at work. There once came a man, a man called Jesus, to Bethlehem and Nazareth and Jerusalem. People watched him at work. His hand reached out to all in need. He was stopped by sickness, he was halted by sorrow, he was oppressed by anxiety, he was challenged by death. So, where ever he went, Jesus reached out a hand in blessing.

Presently men began to say, this is not a man only, this is God. This is the hand of God. So ever since, because we saw God in one moment of time, we believe that all moments of time are filled with a caring God. God came to one place called Bethlehem, and now we meet him in all places everywhere. He touched in love individuals in the first century. So he cares for individual people in all centuries.

A Christian is somebody who looks back that he might look forward. We have faith because once God has acted. We know forever what he is like. So we accept the words of Jesus: "Be not anxious, for your heavenly Father knows that you have need of all these things. Faith has substance, the substance of an historic event; the life, the death, the resurrection of Jesus.

God is a factor, the unknown element in every situation. This is part of the substance of faith. God is at work in his world. Only, often, as we look back, do we see what he has been doing.

I can look back now over fifteen years of ministry in the Sydney Central Methodist Mission. I see the way, year by year, God has opened doors to new ways of serving this city. One by one, homes and hospitals have been added. We have seen the miracle of the telephone ministry called Life Line and now the wonder of our country center for everybody, Vision Valley. As we recall what God has done, the way money has flowed in, the obstacles that have been overcome, the people who have given themselves in dedication, we see again and again something happening beyond all our dreams or expectations.

Let me recount a personal story. As I look back over my own life, I am amazed at the evidence of the leading of God. In the mid-fifties, I was the leader of the Mission to the Nation in Australia and then was invited to America to conduct a Mission to America. When this was over, my hope was to return to Australia. However, nothing seemed to open and I wondered what I should do. We were cast into doubt and uncertainty. Then came an invitation to accept one of the great churches of America, and the temptation was severe. Yet, somehow I felt that it was not God's will that we should remain there.

So in faith, not knowing where we were going, we set off homeward. On the return journey, I preached in England. One day, while missioning in the Doncaster coalfields, there came an excited telephone call from my wife. She told me that a cable had just arrived. "Central Methodist Mission, Sydney, unexpectedly opening, expect invitation." We returned to Sydney and to the mission, which I believe was God's appointment for my life.

As I look back, I think God was there, the unknown factor, causing us to reject that opening in America, bringing us home, though we did not know where we were going or why we should return. This was God, the unknown factor, guiding in the small affairs of one family. There is substance to faith and evidence of the unseen in God's action in human affairs.

The substance of faith is seen on the vast canvas of

history. We sometimes imagine that the world is man's alone.

I like the cartoon that appeared as a commentary on world leaders' summit actions. There was God in heaven, with the angel Gabriel getting ready to blow a huge trumpet. God seemed to be planning to wind up history, to bring the sorry human drama to an end. God takes a last look down from heaven and shouts: "Hold it, Gabriel. They are going to have another summit meeting."

History does not belong to man. God is always the unknown factor in every age. I know we must be concerned about pollution, we must worry about the atomic bomb, we must face the population explosion. However, I often think the dire prophecies of scientists and others forget there is another factor in the picture, God.

In Auckland, New Zealand, there is a monument to the Maori people. It commemorates the relationship between the Maoris and the white people. At one time, it was not meant to be that kind of monument. Back in the last century, when the Maori race seemed rapidly to be dying out, someone left a fortune to set up a monument when the last Maori died. It was to be a monument to an extinct race. Then the man who bequeathed his fortune died, but the Maoris decided to live. The birthrate went up. Now there are more Maoris than ever.

Do you really think God is going to permit this world to be polluted out of existence? Do you think he is overlooking the population explosion? Do you imagine God will allow any nation completely to destroy the earth by atomic power?

What I am trying to say is: First, let us introduce some calmness and balance in all the alarms of a frightening world. As we rightfully and urgently struggle against pollution, the population expansion, and the atomic bomb, let us remember we do not struggle alone. There is an unknown factor, it is God. This is our heavenly Father's world. "Faith is the substance of things hoped for, the evidence of things not seen."

There is substance to faith in surrendering our lives to God's will and purpose. Faith is surrender. Walking by faith means giving ourselves over freely and trustingly to God.

There are two ways of living. One way is to make our own choices, to be quite specific about what we want to do and be, to select our own goals, to spend our days carving out a niche for ourselves in the world.

A second way is to open ourselves freely to the future. It is to be less specific in our ambitions, to believe that we will find fulfillment for our existence even though we cannot quite see what it will be. It is to surrender our personal ambition to God's ambition. It is to let him take over, to trust him for the future.

Monica was the mother of Augustine, one of the greatest leaders of the church in the fourth century. Augustine was quite a man. He was a sensualist. By the age of thirty, he had lived with two mistresses, fathered an illegitimate child, become a homosexual. Then he announced to his mother that he was going to Rome. She was panic-stricken. Rome, the very cesspool of vice, was the last place for Augustine to live. This would be the complete undoing of her son. In the end, Augustine lied to his mother and escaped to Rome. What Monica did not know was that Augustine would meet in Rome the great Ambrose, the Bishop of Milan. Through him was released an influence that led to the conversion of Augustine to Christ.

Monica had chosen her own goals saying, "My son must not go to Rome lest he be destroyed." God had other plans. So a mother had her immediate prayer unanswered, but her deepest longing fulfilled. Faith is surrender, surrender to God's plans and purposes.

God is ever working for our true fulfillment. The substance of our faith is that God craves the best for us and works to bring it about.

God never lets up with you, he never lets up with me. When we sin, he follows us with forgiveness. When we are plagued by guilt, he offers his pardon. When we are tempted to the breaking point, he touches us in strength. When we make a mess of his world, he starts to build it again in peace and justice.

God has his dreams for society, for the world, for history. Running through the Bible, there is a wonderful picture of a world at peace, even the peace of nature. In the book of Isaiah we read: "The wolf shall dwell with the lamb, and the leopard shall lie down with the kid, and the calf and the lion and the fatling together; and a little child shall lead them." And in Colossians we read that through Christ, God will reconcile all things to himself, "whether on earth or in heaven, making peace by the blood of his cross." Oh, God has a wonderful dream of perfection, of fulfillment, for mankind and for natural creation. This is the substance of our faith.

God, in Jesus, is ever leading onward. He is ready to disclose himself and his purposes to us. He asks us to seek to understand his plans for the future and to make them our own. Our task is to find out what he is doing and to do it with him. Faith is surrender to the dreams of God.

Many believe that the Spanish explorer Pedro de Queiros was the discoverer of Australia. It happened this way.

Pedro de Queiros became convinced that somewhere beyond the horizon was a great southern continent. With two vessels, he set out from South America. Sailing on, he came to the islands off the Australian coast and saw the long shoreline of a large land mass in the distance.

A mighty storm blew up and the two ships were separated. Frustrated, Pedro de Queiros was forced to return to Mexico.

From 1606 to 1614, de Queiros tried to convince the Spanish authorities in South America that there was a southern continent and that it should be annexed by Spain. He journeyed to Spain, asking that an expedition be formed to claim the land.

No one believed him. Other explorers poured scorn on his claim. There is no southern continent, they said. No one would listen to him. Still Pedro de Queiros gave his answer, "There is a great southern continent. I know there is. I have seen it."

There are many today who say there is no God. They deny that Jesus Christ calls us to a great future, with faith not fear leading onward. There is only one answer to give: There is a God. I know there is. I have seen Him.

So, let me ask, how are you handling the future? Are you walking in dread, tearful of tomorrow? There is a better way; it is to walk by faith, based on what we have learned about Jesus. It is to hand over our hopes, our dreams to a God who cares. It is to discover the peace which comes when faith is surrender. "Faith is the substance of things hoped for, the evidence of things not seen."